스포츠 영어회화

Sports English Conversation
스포츠 영어회화 3판

편저자 / 박진성 · 문한식

발행일 / 2020년 3월 10일
발행인 / 이광호
발행처 / 대한미디어
등록번호 / 제2-4035호
전　화 / (02) 2267-9731
팩　스 / (02) 2271-1469
홈페이지 / www.daehanmedia.com

ISBN 978-89-5654-498-4 (93690)
정가 18,000원

※ 잘못 만들어진 책은 구입처 및 본사에서 교환해 드립니다.
※ 이 책의 저작권은 저자에게 있으며, 저작권법에 의해 보호받는
　 저작물이므로 무단으로 전재하거나 복제하여 사용할 수 없습니다.

스포츠 영어회화 3판

박진성·문한식 편저

Contents

서문

I. BASIC SPOKEN ENGLISH ⋯⋯⋯⋯⋯⋯⋯⋯⋯⋯⋯⋯⋯⋯⋯⋯⋯⋯⋯⋯⋯⋯⋯ 11

    1. Self-Introduction ⋯⋯⋯⋯⋯⋯⋯⋯⋯⋯⋯⋯⋯⋯⋯⋯⋯⋯⋯⋯⋯⋯ 13
    2. About You & Me ⋯⋯⋯⋯⋯⋯⋯⋯⋯⋯⋯⋯⋯⋯⋯⋯⋯⋯⋯⋯⋯⋯ 18
    3. Variety of Dialogues ⋯⋯⋯⋯⋯⋯⋯⋯⋯⋯⋯⋯⋯⋯⋯⋯⋯⋯⋯⋯⋯ 22
    4. Asking Questions ⋯⋯⋯⋯⋯⋯⋯⋯⋯⋯⋯⋯⋯⋯⋯⋯⋯⋯⋯⋯⋯⋯ 25
    5. Asking for Help ⋯⋯⋯⋯⋯⋯⋯⋯⋯⋯⋯⋯⋯⋯⋯⋯⋯⋯⋯⋯⋯⋯⋯ 28
    6. Making Suggestions ⋯⋯⋯⋯⋯⋯⋯⋯⋯⋯⋯⋯⋯⋯⋯⋯⋯⋯⋯⋯⋯ 31
    7. Expressions of Feeling ⋯⋯⋯⋯⋯⋯⋯⋯⋯⋯⋯⋯⋯⋯⋯⋯⋯⋯⋯⋯⋯ 34
    8. Expressing Thanks ⋯⋯⋯⋯⋯⋯⋯⋯⋯⋯⋯⋯⋯⋯⋯⋯⋯⋯⋯⋯⋯⋯ 40
    9. Making Apologies ⋯⋯⋯⋯⋯⋯⋯⋯⋯⋯⋯⋯⋯⋯⋯⋯⋯⋯⋯⋯⋯⋯ 42

II. EVERYDAY ENGLISH ⋯⋯⋯⋯⋯⋯⋯⋯⋯⋯⋯⋯⋯⋯⋯⋯⋯⋯⋯⋯⋯⋯⋯ 45

    1. Greetings ⋯⋯⋯⋯⋯⋯⋯⋯⋯⋯⋯⋯⋯⋯⋯⋯⋯⋯⋯⋯⋯⋯⋯⋯⋯⋯ 47
    2. Weather ⋯⋯⋯⋯⋯⋯⋯⋯⋯⋯⋯⋯⋯⋯⋯⋯⋯⋯⋯⋯⋯⋯⋯⋯⋯⋯⋯ 55
    3. Time & Date ⋯⋯⋯⋯⋯⋯⋯⋯⋯⋯⋯⋯⋯⋯⋯⋯⋯⋯⋯⋯⋯⋯⋯⋯⋯ 62
    4. Emotions ⋯⋯⋯⋯⋯⋯⋯⋯⋯⋯⋯⋯⋯⋯⋯⋯⋯⋯⋯⋯⋯⋯⋯⋯⋯⋯ 69
    5. Telephone ⋯⋯⋯⋯⋯⋯⋯⋯⋯⋯⋯⋯⋯⋯⋯⋯⋯⋯⋯⋯⋯⋯⋯⋯⋯⋯ 77
    6. Hobbies ⋯⋯⋯⋯⋯⋯⋯⋯⋯⋯⋯⋯⋯⋯⋯⋯⋯⋯⋯⋯⋯⋯⋯⋯⋯⋯⋯ 86
    7. Invitation & Visit ⋯⋯⋯⋯⋯⋯⋯⋯⋯⋯⋯⋯⋯⋯⋯⋯⋯⋯⋯⋯⋯⋯⋯ 94
    8. Opinions ⋯⋯⋯⋯⋯⋯⋯⋯⋯⋯⋯⋯⋯⋯⋯⋯⋯⋯⋯⋯⋯⋯⋯⋯⋯⋯ 102
    9. Health ⋯⋯⋯⋯⋯⋯⋯⋯⋯⋯⋯⋯⋯⋯⋯⋯⋯⋯⋯⋯⋯⋯⋯⋯⋯⋯⋯ 110
    10. School ⋯⋯⋯⋯⋯⋯⋯⋯⋯⋯⋯⋯⋯⋯⋯⋯⋯⋯⋯⋯⋯⋯⋯⋯⋯⋯⋯ 118
    11. Restaurant ⋯⋯⋯⋯⋯⋯⋯⋯⋯⋯⋯⋯⋯⋯⋯⋯⋯⋯⋯⋯⋯⋯⋯⋯⋯ 126
    12. Shopping ⋯⋯⋯⋯⋯⋯⋯⋯⋯⋯⋯⋯⋯⋯⋯⋯⋯⋯⋯⋯⋯⋯⋯⋯⋯⋯ 134
    13. Directions ⋯⋯⋯⋯⋯⋯⋯⋯⋯⋯⋯⋯⋯⋯⋯⋯⋯⋯⋯⋯⋯⋯⋯⋯⋯ 142
    14. Traveling ⋯⋯⋯⋯⋯⋯⋯⋯⋯⋯⋯⋯⋯⋯⋯⋯⋯⋯⋯⋯⋯⋯⋯⋯⋯⋯ 149
    15. Sports ⋯⋯⋯⋯⋯⋯⋯⋯⋯⋯⋯⋯⋯⋯⋯⋯⋯⋯⋯⋯⋯⋯⋯⋯⋯⋯⋯ 158

    우리의 생활에서 스포츠는 숲속 산소와 같은 활력소가 된다. 오늘날 스포츠는 스포츠맨이든 아니든 간에 스포츠를 즐기지 않는 사람이 거의 없을 만큼 생활의 일부가 되었다. 가까이 하면 할수록 일상생활이 그만큼 힘을 받는다.

    이러한 실상은 스포츠가 국내의 행사로만 국한되지 않고 가까운 친목모임에서부터 스포츠 외교를 비롯한 국가 간의 각종 스포츠 이벤트는 물론 올림픽 경기에 이르기까지 더욱 다채로워지고 점점 심화되어 간다. 월드컵이나 세계야구대회(WBC)가 전 지구촌의 축제인 것은 이를 잘 말해준다.

    이렇듯 스포츠에 대한 관심은 빈번한 국제경기대회에서 의사소통능력 신장이 주요 요건임을 재인식하게 한다. 더구나 체육인에게는 국제경기대회를 운영하고 관리할 책무가 맡겨져 있기도 하다. 따라서 스포츠를 전공하는 학생은 말할 나위 없이 스포츠 영어의 학습이 필수적이다.

    뿐만 아니라, 영어를 배우고자 하는 일반 학생들도 생활 속의 스포츠를 통하여 영어회화를 익히는 것이 가장 효율적인 방법의 하나라고 생각한다. 스포츠가 서로 간에 직접적인 관련이 없고 공동의 취미활동이 아니라 하더라도 거의 누구에게나 원활한 의사소통의 소재가 되기 때문이다.

    따라서 본 저자는 스포츠 관계자뿐만 아니라 스포츠 관련 분야에서 활동하고

III. SPORTS ACTIVITIES ... 167

1. Sporting Spirit ... 169
2. Baseball ... 174
3. Swimming ... 179
4. Basketball ... 184
5. Volleyball ... 190
6. Soccer ... 195
7. American Football ... 203
8. Camping ... 208
9. Tennis ... 213
10. Mountaineering ... 218
11. Skiing ... 223
12. Skating ... 228
13. Golf ... 233
14. The Olympics ... 238

IV. ATTENDANCE IN THE OLYMPICS ... 247

1. Briefing and Business ... 249
2. Access Control ... 257
3. Check-in and Check-out ... 260
4. At a Lodging Area ... 265
5. At the Information Center ... 267
6. International Cooperation ... 272
7. The Flag Raising Ceremony ... 274
8. Meal Service ... 282
9. The Amenities ... 284
10. Games Management ... 300
11. At the International Airport ... 308
12. On the Playing Field ... 312
13. In a Team Bus ... 316
14. At the Ticket Office ... 321
15. In the Hotel Lobby ... 323

참고문헌
저자소개

자 하는 영어 학도들을 위하여 이 책을 쓰게 되었다. 그동안 스포츠 영어 수업 시간에 다루었던 강의 자료를 중심으로 스포츠와 관련된 내용을 **총 4단원으로** 나누었으며,

단원 I에서는 외국인을 만났을 때 말문트기 기초영어회화편을 준비하였고, 단원 II에서는 길안내 등 일상적인 기초대화편을 준비하였다. 단원 III에서는 주로 학교 스포츠로 다루는 스포츠 종목 관련 기사를 실어 실용 스포츠 영어를 익히도록 하였다. 단원 IV에서는 올림픽 경기와 같은 국제 경기 상황에서 발생하는 내용을 예시함으로써 국제경기대회의 이해를 돕고자 하였다.

특히, 이번 개정판에서는 내용을 수정·보완하고 대화문은 한글을 바로 영어로 통역할 수 있도록 한영대역으로 편집하여 학습의 효율성을 높이고자 하였다. 우리는 흔히 웬만큼 영어를 해석할 수는 있으나 한글을 영어로 옮기는 능력은 많이 부족한 편이다. 바로 한글 내용을 영어로 옮기는 연습이야말로 통역의 기초가 되므로, 이러한 방법으로 꾸준히 학습하기를 권장한다.

스포츠 전문용어가 주로 영어인 것을 감안하면 스포츠를 중심으로 한 영어회화는 영어와 스포츠를 함께 공부할 수 있는 일석이조가 될 것이다. 요컨대, 영어 의사소통능력이 절실하고 국제경기대회가 늘어가고 있는 현대사회에서 스포츠 행사의 개요, 지원 및 참가 등을 위한 스포츠 현장 중심의 의사소통능력을 신장하는 데 이 책이 요긴하게 쓰이길 바란다.

2018년 9월

대표저자 **박 진 성**

I. Basic Spoken English

1. Self-Introduction

2. About You & Me

3. Variety of Dialogues

4. Asking Questions

5. Asking for Help

6. Making Suggestions

7. Expressions of Feeling

8. Expressing Thanks

9. Making Apologies

1. Self-Introduction

Basic Pattern

1. 자기 소개 (Self-Introduction)

1) 저의 이름은 김진호입니다.
   My name is Jin-ho Kim.

2) 저는 24살입니다.
   I am 24 **years old**.

3) 서울에서 태어났고 자랐습니다. 순천대학교 4학년 학생이며, 오는 2월에 사회체육학과의 이학사 학위를 받을 예정입니다.
   I **was born and raised** in Seoul.
   I am a senior student of Sunchon National University. And this coming February I'll get **a Bachelor of Science** in Sport and Leisure Science.

4) 저는 국가대표 팀 소속입니다.
   I am **on** the Korean national **team**.

5) 저는 육상선수입니다.
   I am **a track and field athlete**.

2. 나의 가족 (My Family)

1) 가족은 4명인데 부모님, 누이 1명, 그리고 저입니다.
   There are four members in my family; my parents, one sister, and myself.

2) 아버지는 서울에서 회사에 다니십니다.

I. Basic Spoken English

My father **works for** a company in Seoul.

3) 어머니는 전업주부이시고, 제 누이는 학생입니다.

My mother is **a housewife**, and my sister is a student.

4) 우리 모두는 서로 대화를 즐깁니다. 특히 식사 때에는 함께 모여 식사하면서 대화를 합니다.

We all **enjoy talking** to each other, especially at meal times. We all **get together** to eat and talk.

5) 우리 집에서는 대화가 활발합니다.

We talk very **lively** at our home.(Our family is very conversational.)

3. 취 미 (Hobbies)

1) 저는 케이 팝 음악 듣기를 좋아 합니다.

I like **listening to** K-pop music.

2) 저는 여행을 아주 좋아하며 할 수 있는 대로 많이 여행합니다.

I love traveling and I travel **as often as I can**.

3) 저는 거의 모든 운동을 즐기지만, 특히 테니스를 좋아합니다.

I **enjoy** almost all sports.

I especially like tennis.

4) 저는 또한 대학에서 테니스 클럽의 회원이기도 합니다.

I'm also **a member of** the tennis club in college.

5) 테니스는 신체 내의 모든 근육을 써야 하기 때문에 제 건강을 유지시켜 줍니다.

Tennis **keeps** me **fit** because I have to use every muscle in my body.

6) 테니스를 힘들여 잘 치고 난 후 맥주 한 잔의 맛은 훨씬 더 좋습니다.

A glass of cool beer tastes so **much better** after a hard game of tennis.

4. 성격 (Character)

1) 저는 일에 매우 열정적으로 접근한다고 생각합니다.
   I think I **approach things** very enthusiastically.

2) 저는 어떤 일을 어중간하게 남겨두는 걸 싫어합니다.
   I don't like to **leave** any**thing half-done**.

3) 일을 하다가 중간에 그만 두게 되면, 거기에 신경이 쓰여 견딜 수가 없습니다.
   It **makes me nervous**. I can't **concentrate on** anything else until the first thing is finished.

4) 저는 주위의 사람들과 어울리고 함께 일하기를 좋아합니다.
   I like **being around** people and doing things with people.

5) 그래서 외향적이라 말할 수 있다고 생각합니다.
   So, I guess you**'d** say I'm **rather** extroverted(outgoing).

5. 장점과 약점 (Strength and Weakness)

1) 사람들은 내가 돈 안 되는 일만 한다고들 합니다.
   People say that I always do things that are not going to make any money.

2) 저는 다른 사람들이 성가셔 하는 일을 떠맡을 수 있고, 될 때까지 그저 천천히 일해 나갑니다.
   I **take on** jobs that bother other people and just work at them slowly until they get done.

3) 그렇게 하는 것을 좋아하고, 그게 저의 좋은 점이라고 생각합니다.
   I enjoy **that sort of thing** - that's my strong point, I suppose.

I. Basic Spoken English

4) 저는 밖으로 나가서 다른 사람들과 더 어울리고 싶고, 그런 일을 하고 있습니다.

I enjoy going out and getting along with people. I would like to do that kind of work in the future.

Oral Drill

1. I'm <u>Min-su Hwang from Korea.</u>
    a student of Sunchon National University
    a volunteer of the Gwangju Universiade

2. I was <u>born in Seoul.</u>
    born in 1999
    raised in Busan

3. There are <u>four members in my family.</u>
    many books in the room
    four distinct seasons in Korea
    a lot of places to visit around here

4. My hobby is <u>listening to music.</u>
    taking a walk
    collecting stamps
    going to the movies
    playing computer games

5. I have been <u>studying English for seven years.</u>
    staying here since last week
    getting along with him recently
    living in Gwangju for three years

I. **Basic Spoken English**

2. About You & Me

Basic Pattern

1. 대화를 시작할 때 (Starting Dialogue)

1) 잠깐 실례해도 될까요?
   May I interrupt for a moment?

2) 잠깐만 말씀드릴 수 있을까요?
   Can I talk to you for a few minutes?

3) 제가 당신께 말씀드릴 기회를 가질 수 있을까 싶습니다.
   I wonder if I could have a chance to talk to you?

4) 잠깐 시간 좀 내 주실래요?
   Can you **spare me a minute**?

5) 뭔가를 말씀드릴까 합니다.
   Let me tell you something.

2. 외모와 성격 (Appearance & Personality)

1) 그는 어떻게 생겼는가요?
   What does he look like?

2) 당신은 키도 크고 미남이십니다.
   You're **tall** and **handsome**.

3) 그녀는 긴 곱슬머리를 하고 있습니다.
   She has long **curly hair**.

4) 당신은 지난번 본 이후로 체중이 빠졌네요.

You've **lost weight** since I saw you last.

5) 그는 어떤 사람이에요?

What kind of person is he?

6) 그는 영리하기도 하지만 다정해요.

He is not only **smart**, but **friendly** too.

7) 그녀는 항상 어려운 사람을 도와줍니다.

She always **helps people in trouble**.

8) 저는 너무 부끄러워해서 여러 사람 앞에서 말을 잘 못합니다.

I am too **shy** to speak in front of people.

3. 습 관 (Habits)

1) 저는 손톱 깨무는 버릇이 있습니다.

I **have a habit of biting my nails**.

2) 저는 가끔 숙제를 미루곤 합니다.

I often **put off doing** my homework.

3) 나쁜 습관을 없애기는 어렵습니다.

It is hard to **break** bad **habits**.

4) 저는 보통 텔레비전 보느라고 늦게까지 앉아 있곤 합니다.

I usually **stay up late watching** TV.

5) 저는 항상 잘 기억하려고 메모를 합니다.

I always **take notes** to remember things well.

I. Basic Spoken English

4. 대화에 반응할 때 (Dialogue Responses)

1) 확실합니다.
   Absolutely.

2) 아, 그런가요?
   Oh, **do you**?

3) 두 말할 나위없지요.
   You can say that **again**.

4) 제 말도 그렇지요.
   I feel the same.

5) 저는 그렇게 생각 않는데요.
   I don't think so.

6) 다시 한 번 말씀해 주시겠어요?
   I beg your **pardon**, sir?

7) 그게 무슨 말씀인가요?
   What do you **mean** by that?

8) 말씀하신 요지를 알겠어요.
   I **do understand** your point.

9) 저는 그 말씀을 전혀 모르겠어요.
   I can't understand at all.

Oral Drill

1. I'll <u>travel</u> to China.
    take a trip
    go on a trip

2. What do you do <u>on Sundays?</u>
            as a hobby
            in your free time
            during the weekend

3. I usually <u>listen to K-pop</u>.
        watch movies
        play soccer with my friends

4. I <u>like</u> it.
    love
    really like
    kind of like

5. I <u>don't like</u> it.
    hate
    don't really like

6. I hear <u>you</u> are interested in <u>music</u>.
        he is   soccer
        she is   dancing

3. Variety of Dialogues

Basic Pattern

1. 다양한 대화 (Variety of Dialogues)

1) 탁자 위에 책 한 권이 있습니다.
   There is a book on the table.

2) 문에 뭔가가 있습니다.
   There is something at the door.

3) 공원에 꽃이 많이 있습니까?
   Are there **lots of flowers** in the park?

4) 저는 제 책이 어디 있는지 모르겠네요.
   I don't know **where my book is**.

5) 언덕 위의 구름 좀 보세요.
   Look at the cloud above the hill.

6) 이게 당신의 휴대폰인가요? - 네, 그렇습니다.
   Is this **your cell phone**? - Yes, **it**'s mine.

7) 언덕 위의 그 집은 저의 삼촌 댁입니다.
   The house on the hill is my **uncle's**.

2. 다양한 상황 (Diverse Situations)

1) 그것은 당신에게 달렸어요.
   It**'s up to** you.

I. Basic Spoken English

2) 저는 괜찮아요.

   It **doesn't matter** to me.

3) 새 차를 구하셨네요.

   You have a **brand-new** car.

4) 옷을 제대로 차려 입으셨습니다.

   You're all **dressed up**.

5) 나이에 비해 젊어 보이세요.

   You **look young** for your age.

6) 그들 중 두, 셋은 낯이 익네요.

   Two or three of them **look familiar**.

7) 여기에는 그런 이름 가진 분이 없어요.

   There is **no one here** by that name.

8) 저 분들 중 어느 분이 테일러 씨인가요?

   Which one of those men is Mr. Taylor?

9) 그런데 당신은 누굴 기다리고 있나요?

   By the way, **who** are you **waiting for**?

10) 그들은 정말로 닮았어요.

    They really **look alike**.

I. Basic Spoken English

Oral Drill

1. There is <u>a book</u> on the table.
    - a vase
    - are a few dishes
    - are forks and knives

2. I don't know where <u>my book</u> is.
    - your CD
    - his pencils are
    - her friends are

3. Does this <u>radio</u> belong to you?
    - phone
    - jacket
    - Do these pictures

4. You have <u>an iPad</u>, don't you?
    - a big family
    - a phonograph
    - 2 cute puppies

5. Whose coat is this? - It's <u>mine</u>.
    - his
    - hers
    - my uncle's

4. Asking Questions

Basic Pattern

1. Yes-No 의문문 (Yes-No Question)

1) 당신은 한국인인가요?

   Are you Korean?

2) 당신은 아침에 일찍 일어납니까?

   Do you get up early in the morning?

3) 그 경기가 흥미진진하던가요?

   Were you excited by the game?

4) 당신은 그들과 재미있게 보내셨어요?

   Did you have a good time with them?

5) 당신은 커피나 오렌지 주스를 좋아하세요?

   Do you like coffee or orange juice?

6) 우유 드시겠어요?

   Would you like some milk?

7) 테니스 잘 치신가요?

   Can you play tennis very well?

8) 창문 좀 열어주실 수 있어요?

   Could you open the window?

9) 저를 도와주시겠어요?

   Will you give me a hand?

2. Wh-의문문 (Wh-Question)

1) 저기 저 남자가 누구인가요?

   Who is the man over there?

2) 누구한테 투표하시겠어요?

   Who will you vote for?

3) 어떤 회사에 근무하세요?

   What company do you work for?

4) 직업이 뭔가요?

   What do you do for a living?

5) 고향이 어디세요?

   Where do you come from?

6) 당신 어제 어디 가셨어요?

   Where did you go yesterday?

7) 언제 런던으로 떠나시나요?

   When are you leaving for London?

8) 언제 태어났어요?

   When were you born?

9) 거기에 무얼 타고 갔어요?

   How did you go there?

10) 체중이 얼마예요?

   How much do you weigh?

Oral Drill

1. Would you like <u>some milk</u>?
            some ketchup
            some sausages

2. <u>Yes, please</u>.
   No, thank you.
   That'd be great, thanks.

3. Do you <u>play soccer</u>?
            go to church on Sundays
            get up early in the morning
            do your homework every evening

4. Where <u>are you from</u>?
            do you come from
            did you go last weekend

5. How <u>old are you</u>?
       big is your family
       much did you pay for it

6. What <u>do you do</u> on Sunday?
        are you going to do
        did you go there for

5. Asking for Help

Basic Pattern

1. 부탁 (Asking for a Favor)

1) 부탁 좀 할 수 있을까요?
   Can I ask you for a favor?

2) 저를 도와주시겠습니까?
   Would you do me a favor?

3) 저를 도와주시면 어떨까요?
   Would you mind helping me?

4) 저에게 도움을 주시겠습니까?
   Could you **give me a hand**?

5) 저에게 뭔가 해주실 수 있겠어요?
   Could you do **something for me**?

2. 길 묻기 (Asking the Way)

1) 미안합니다만, 저는 여기가 초행입니다.
   I'm sorry, but I'm a stranger here myself.

2) 시티 파크로 가는 길을 안내해 주시겠습니까?
   Would you show me the way to the City Park?

3) 한국은행으로 어떻게 가죠?
   How do I get to the Bank of Korea?

4) 국립박물관을 찾고 있습니다. 어디에 있죠?

   I'm **look**ing **for** the National Museum. Where is it?

5) 여기서 역까지는 얼마나 멉니까?

   How far is it from here to the station?

6) 당신께 지도를 그려드릴까요?

   Shall I **draw a map** for you?

7) 이 근처에 공중전화가 있을까요?

   Is there a pay-phone around here?

8) 이 길이 버스터미널로 가는 지름길입니까?

   Is this **the shortest way to** the bus terminal?

3. 기타 요청 (Asking the Others)

1) 시간 좀 할애해 주시겠습니까?

   Can you **spare** me a moment of your time?

2) 이것 좀 들어 주시겠습니까?

   Would you **hold** this for me?

3) 제 가방 지켜봐 주시겠습니까?

   Would you **keep an eye** on my bag?

4) 여유 돈이 있으신가요?

   Do you have any **money to spare**?

I. Basic Spoken English

Oral Drill

1. Could you <u>do me a favor</u>?
          give her a message
          have her call me back
          open the window? It's too hot for me.

2. <u>Sure</u>.
   No problem
   Sure, I'll give it to her right away
   Yes, of course. I'll be glad to. (I'm sorry, but ….)

3. Do you mind <u>if I open the window</u>?
          if I turn on the TV
          if I smoke

4. I'm afraid <u>you may catch a cold</u>.
          I can't go with you
          he may fail in the business

5. Please don't <u>bother</u> me now, I'm very busy.
          talk to
          interrupt
          argue with

6. If you have time, will you <u>call me</u> tomorrow?
          help him
          join them

6. Making Suggestions

Basic Pattern

1. 제 안 (Suggestions)

1) 저는 그게 괜찮다고 봅니다.
   I think it's all right.

2) 당신은 그의 말을 들어야 해요.
   You should listen to him.

3) 당신은 담배를 끊는 게 좋겠어요.
   You'd better quit smoking.

4) 당신은 집에 있는 편이 낫겠어요.
   You might as well stay home.

5) 저는 우리가 그에게 이 문제에 대하여 이야기할 것을 제안합니다.
   I suggest we speak to him about this matter.

6) 만일 제가 당신이라면 나는 그의 제의를 수용하겠습니다.
   If I were you, **I would** accept his offer.

2. 동의 요청 (Request for Agreement)

1) 당신이 반대 안하신다면, 그것을 열심히 하겠어요.
   If you have no objection, I'll go for it.

2) 괜찮으시다면, 창문을 열게요.
   If you don't mind, let me open the window.

3) 당신이 좋으시면, 그걸로 결정합시다.

If it's all right with you, let's make a decision.

4) 당신이 좋다면, 제가 대신 거기에 가겠어요.

I'll go there instead of you, **if you like**.

5) 제가 커튼을 올릴까요?

Would you like me to pull up the curtains?

3. 권 유 (Solicitation)

1) 드라이브하러 가는 게 어때요?

How about going for a drive?

2) 맥주 한 잔 어떻습니까?

Would you like a beer?

3) 쇼핑하러 갑시다.

Let's go shopping.

4) 여기서 기다리는 것이 어떨까요?

Why don't we wait here.

5) 괜찮으시다면 저희와 함께 가시죠?

You're welcome to join us, **if you want**.

6) 우리 톰에게 잠깐 들렀다 갈까요?

Shall we drop in on Tom?

Oral Drill

1. <u>Let's</u> have lunch with him today.
   Won't you
   Why don't you
   How about having
   What do you say to having lunch

2. You'd better <u>hurry home</u>.
       start right now
       tell your mother
       phone home first

3. In my opinion, that's <u>an excellent</u> idea.
         a good
         a wonderful
         a marvelous

4. What do you think of <u>my son</u>?
         my pet dog
         his garden
         his story
         her poem

5. I will open the window, <u>if you like</u>.
         if you want
         if you don't mind

7. Expressions of Feeling

Basic Pattern

1. 기 쁨 (Pleasure)

1) (왕처럼) 아주 행복합니다.

   I'm as happy as a king.

2) 콧노래가 절로 납니다.

   I feel like humming.

3) 경기에 우승하셨다니 매우 기쁩니다.

   I'm so glad you won the game.

4) 우리가 해냈어.

   We made it.

5) 매우 기쁘시겠습니다.

   You must be very pleased.

6) 그 말을 들으니 기쁩니다.

   I'm delighted to hear that.

7) 이렇게 즐거울 수가 없어요.

   Nothing gives me so much pleasure.

2. 칭 찬 (Praise)

1) 참 잘 했어요.

   You did a good job.

2) 당신이 그렇게 잘 하리라 기대하지 않았습니다.
I didn't expect you to do such **a good job**.

3) 새 셔츠를 입으니 멋져 보입니다.
You look nice in your new shirt.

4) 나이에 비해 젊어 보이십니다.
You look young **for your age**.

5) 당신은 이 사진에 아름답게 나왔네요.
You look **beautiful** in this picture.

6) 그 분은 진정 신사이십니다.
He's a gentleman **in every sense of the word**.

3. 놀 람 (Surprise)

1) 놀랐는걸(깜짝이야)!
What a surprise!

2) 그건 믿어지지 않아!
That's incredible!

3) 그의 말에 충격을 받았어요.
His words **shocked me**.

4) 매우 긴장되네요.
I'm **so nervous**.

5) 진정하십시오!
Please **calm down**!

I. Basic Spoken English

4. 슬 픔 (Sorrows)

1) 그는 괴로워하고 있어요.
   He has been feeling **down**.

2) 저는 그럴 기분이 아니에요.
   I'm not **in the mood for** that.

3) 무슨 일이야? 안 좋아 보여.
   What's up? You look down.

4) 저는 비참하네요.
   I feel miserable.

5) 그녀의 죽음이 정말 내 가슴을 미어지게 했어요.
   Her death really **broke my heart**.

5. 두려움 (Fear)

1) 그 생각만 하면 무섭습니다.
   I **dread to** think of it.

2) 그것 때문에 소름이 끼쳤습니다.
   That gave me the creeps/shivers.

3) 너무 놀라서 움직일 수가 없었습니다.
   I was **too** shocked **to** move.

4) 등골에 땀이 나요.
   I **have perspiration** on my back.

5) 무서워서 죽을 뻔했어요.
   I was **scared to death**.

6) 그는 고소공포증이 있습니다.
He has **a fear of** heights.

6. 격 려 (Encouragement)

1) 힘을 내요.
Cheer up!

2) 한국, 파이팅!
Way to **go**! Korea.

3) 자, 당신은 할 수 있어요.
Come on, you can do that.

4) 참 잘 했어요. 당신이 자랑스럽네요.
You did a **good job**. I'm **proud of** you.

5) 다음번엔 더 열심히 하세요.
Try harder next time.

6) 당신이 못하면 누가 해요?
If you can't do it, who else?

Basic Spoken English

Oral Drill

1. You look <u>happy all the time</u>.
         nice in your new dress
         wonderful with that hairdo

2. You <u>praise me too much</u>.
       make me blush
       are flattering me

3. I am as <u>happy</u> as a <u>king</u>.
       busy   bee
       hungry hawk
       cheerful lark
       proud   peacock

4. I was <u>delighted</u> to hear the news.
       pleased
       surprised
       disappointed

5. I was <u>scared</u>.
       scared to death
       too shocked to move

6. What a <u>surprise</u>!
       shame
       relief

7. <u>Well done</u>! Now shoot!
   Good job
   That's it

8. Shoot! <u>Take a chance</u>!
   Try it again
   Do your best
   You can do it
   It's now or never
   Pull yourself together

9. Don't <u>worry</u>. I'm sure you'll do better next time.
   give up
   give way to grief
   be too discouraged

10. He was <u>encouraged</u> by those words
    impressed
    inspired
    renewed

11. I'm often <u>at a loss</u>.
    confused
    frustrated
    distracted

8. Expressing Thanks

Basic Pattern

1. 감 사 (Thanks)

1) (태워주셔서) 감사합니다.
   Thank you (for the ride).

2) 큰 도움을 주십니다.
   You're **doing** me a big **favor**.

3) 제 영어 공부를 도와주셔서 감사합니다.
   It's very kind of you to help me with my English.

4) 그 일에 대해 정말로 감사합니다.
   I appreciate it very much.

5) 배려해 주심에 감사드립니다.
   I appreciate your consideration.

6) 제가 보답할 수 있길 바랍니다.
   I hope I can **repay** you **for** it.

7) 저희들은 꼭 그분께 그 일로 감사드려야겠습니다.
   We've got to **thank** him **for** it.

8) 저는 귀하의 호의와 우의에 무척 감사드립니다.
   I appreciate your **hospitality** and friendship very much.

9) 저는 당신과 아주 좋은 시간을 가졌습니다.
   I had a wonderful time being with you.

10) 저는 우리가 함께 했던 매 순간이 아주 즐거웠습니다.
   I've enjoyed every moment we've had together.

11) 더 이상 좋을 수가 없었어요.
   It couldn't be better.

2. 감사에 대한 대답 (Responses to Thanks)

1) 천만에요.
   You're welcome.

2) 그런 말씀 마세요.
   Don't mention it.

3) 똑 같이 당신께도.
   The same to you.

4) 천만에요.
   You're more than welcome.

5) 그렇게 말씀해 주시니 아주 좋습니다.
   It's very nice of you to say so.

6) 제가 기뻤는걸요.
   It was my pleasure.

7) 당신을 도울 수 있어서 너무나 기쁠 따름입니다.
   I'm only **too glad to** be able to help you.

8) 함께 해서 즐거웠습니다.
   I enjoyed your company.

9. Making Apologies

Basic Pattern

1. 사 과 (Apologies)

1) 그 일을 미안하게 생각합니다.
   I feel sorry about it.

2) 사과드릴 게 있습니다.
   I owe you an apology.

3) 그런 일은 다시 일어나지 않도록 하겠습니다.
   It won't happen again.

4) 저의 실수를 사과드립니다.
   I apologize to you for my mistake.

5) 제가 저지른 일에 대해 사과드립니다.
   I apologize for what I've done.

6) 늦어서 미안합니다.
   Excuse me for being late.

7) 기다리게 해서 미안합니다.
   I'm sorry to have kept you waiting.

8) 기다리게 한 점을 용서하십시오.
   Forgive me for making you wait.

2. 폐끼침을 사과함 (Apologies for Bothering)

I. Basic Spoken English

1) 시간을 많이 빼앗지 않았나 싶습니다.
   I'm afraid I've taken up much of your time.

2) 너무 폐를 끼쳐서 죄송합니다.
   I'm sorry to **have troubled you** so much.

3) 불편하게 해드려서 죄송합니다.
   I'm sorry for the inconve- nience.

4) 그런 사고가 난 것은 제 잘못입니다.
   It's my fault that the accident happened.

5) 제가 그런 실수를 한 것은 어리석었습니다.
   It's silly of me to make such a mistake.

6) 제가 잘못한 것이었습니다.
   I was the one **to blame**.

7) 제가 너무 부주의했습니다.
   It was very careless of me.

8) 마음을 상하게 했다면 용서하세요.
   Please **excuse me for** offending you.

9) 고의가 아니었습니다.
   I didn't do it **on purpose**.

10) 의도적은 아니었습니다.
    It wasn't intentional.

11) 당신의 기분을 상하게 하려는 뜻은 아니었습니다.
    I didn't mean to hurt your feelings.

12) 그런 일을 한 것은 제가 경솔했습니다.
    It was hasty of me to do such a thing.

3. 용 서 (Forgiveness)

1) 용서하십시오.
   Forgive me.

2) 한 번 봐 주세요.
   Give me a break, please.

3) 제 사과를 받아주십시오.
   Please accept my apology.

4) 잘못이 있더라도 그를 용서해 주세요.
   Even if there is a mistake, please forgive him.

5) 저를 봐서 그를 용서해 주세요.
   Forgive him for my sake.

6) 저의 무례한 언사를 용서해 주세요.
   Forgive my rude remarks.

7) 한 번 크게 이해해 주세요.
   Please try to understand.

8) 다시는 안 그러겠습니다.
   I won't do it again.

II. Everyday English

1. Greetings
2. Weather
3. Time & Date
4. Emotions
5. Telephone
6. Hobbies
7. Invitation & Visit
8. Opinions
9. Health
10. School
11. Restaurant
12. Shopping
13. Directions
14. Traveling
15. Sports

1. Greetings

Useful Expressions

1. 일상적인 인사

Hi!
Good morning.

2. 근황을 물을 때

How are you?
How are you doing?
How's everything with you?
How are you getting along?

3. 오랜만에 만났을 때

Long time no see.
I haven't seen you for a while.
It's been 3 years since we saw each other.
It seems like ages since I saw you last.
What have you been up to?
I beg your pardon for my long silence.

4. 우연히 만났을 때

What a pleasant surprise!
What a small world!
I never thought I'd run into you here!
You are Jack, aren't you?
Never did I dream of seeing you again.

5. 안부를 전할 때

My husband wants to meet you.
He wanted me to say hello to you.
Mr. Lark gives you his best wishes.
Please give my love to Ruthie.
Please give your wife my regards.

6. 소개할 때

May I introduce myself?
Hello, I don't think we've met before. I'm Jin Kim.
Mr. Park, I'd like you to meet Mr. Kim, our manager.
James, let me introduce my friend Min-su.
It's so nice of you to come. I'm Jin and this is my sister.

7. 초면 인사

How do you do?
Pleased to meet you.
I'm very glad to meet you, Mr. Lee.
I've heard a great deal about you. I've been wanting to meet you.

8. 헤어질 때

It was very nice to meet you.
I enjoyed talking with you.
I hope we'll get the chance to see you again.
Good-bye. I hope I'll see you again soon.
You can always reach me on the phone.
Please let me know what's going on with you.

II. Everyday English

Speaking in English

1) 안녕하세요?

   How are you?

2) 요즘 어떻게 지내세요?

   How are you these days?

3) 부모님들도 잘 계시죠?

   How are your parents?

4) 오늘은 좀 어떠세요?

   How do you feel today?

5) 새로 태어난 기분입니다.

   I feel like a new man/woman.

6) 일은 좀 순조롭게 진행되어 가나요?

   Are you making any progress?

7) 별고 없으십니까?

   What's new?

8) 다시 만나서 반갑습니다.

   It's good to see you again.

9) 요즘 당신 보기 힘들군요.

   I haven't seen much of you lately.

10) 전에 한번 뵌 적이 있는 것 같네요.

    I think I've seen you before.

11) 얼굴이 굉장히 낯이 익은데요.

    Your face is so familiar.

II. Everyday English

12) 광주에서 뵙게 되다니 정말 우연의 일치로군요!
    What a coincidence meeting you in Gwangju!

13) 사람들이 하는 말이 있죠. 세상 참 좁다고요.
    You know what they say, it's a small world!

14) 여길 어떻게 알고 오셨습니까?
    What brought you here?

15) 여기서 당신을 보리라곤 기대하지 않았습니다.
    I didn't expect to see you here.

16) 그냥 인사하려고 들렀어요.
    I just stopped by to say hello.

17) 여름에 어떻게 지내십니까?
    How have you been getting through the hot summer?

18) 어딜 그렇게 쏘다니고 있었니?
    Where have you been hanging around?

19) 어머! 이런데서 너를 만나다니!
    Fancy meeting you are here!

20) 몇 년 만에 만나 뵙는군요.
    I haven't seen you in years.

21) 안녕. 탐, 우연히 만나게 되어 반갑군.
    Hi, Tom. I'm glad I bumped into you.

22) 그렇지 않아도 너를 만나고 싶었었는데.
    You're just the person I wanted to see.

23) 존은 어떻게 됐어요?
    What happened to John?

II. Everyday English

24) 모르겠어요, 하지만 괜찮을 겁니다.
    No news. But I bet he's O.K.

25) 10년 전부터 그와 소식이 끊겼어요.
    I haven't heard from him for 10 years.

26) 얼마나 자주 그의 소식을 듣습니까?
    How often do you hear from him?

27) 그 사람은 건강하게 잘 지냅니다.
    He's in the pink.

28) 이름이 갑자기 생각이 안 나는군요.
    Your name just doesn't come to me.

29) 무엇 때문에 그렇게 바빴어요?
    Why have you been so busy?

30) 당신 가족들은 다 안녕하신지요?
    I hope your family are all well.

31) 미스터 마커스가 안부 전하더군요.
    Mr. Markus sends his regards.

32) 처음 뵙겠습니다. 만나서 반가워요.
    How do you do? I'm glad to meet you.

33) 우리 좋은 친구가 되었으면 합니다.
    I hope we become good fiends.

34) 성함이 어떻게 되시죠?
    May I have your name, please?

35) 가족이 몇 명이나 되세요?
    How large is your family?

II. Everyday English

36) 어디서 오셨습니까? (고향이 어디십니까?)

    Where are you from?

37) 국적이 어디시죠? (어느 나라 분이십니까?)

    What's your nationality?

38) 제 친구 미스터 존슨을 소개 하죠.

    Let me introduce my friend, Mr. Johnson.

39) 스미스 씨, 이분이 미스터 존슨입니다.

    Mr. Smith, this is Mr. Johnson.

40) 전에 한번 뵌 적이 있는 것 같습니다.

    I think I've seen you before.

41) 누구시더라?

    Do I know you?

42) 친숙해 뵈는데요.

    You look very familiar.

43) 예전에 당신을 어디선가 뵌 것 같습니다.

    I am sure I have seen you somewhere before.

44) 우린 종종 당신 이야길 했었지요.

    We have often talked of you.

45) 저 사람이 바로 당신이 말하던 그 사람입니까?

    Is that the man you told me about?

46) 저는 한번 본 사람은 꼭 기억합니다.

    I never forget a face.

47) 분명히 저를 다른 사람과 혼동하셨습니다.

    You must have me mixed up with someone else.

II. Everyday English

48) 성함을 확실히 듣지 못했습 니다.

   I didn't quite catch your name.

49) 죄송합니다. 이름이 뭐라고 하셨는지 잘못 들었습니다.

   I'm sorry. I didn't get your name.

50) 어떻게 부를까요? (성을 부를까요, 이름을 부를까요?)

   How should I address you?(Should I call you by your surname, or your first name?)

51) 준이라고 불러주세요. 그게 제 이름이에요.

   Please call me Joon. That's my first name.

52) 즐거운 하루 보내세요.

   Have a good day.

53) 조심해서 가세요.

   Take care of yourself.

54) 즐거운 여행되시길 바래요.

   Have a good trip!

55) 재미있게 보내라구!

   Enjoy yourself!

56) 좀 더 자주 만납시다.

   Let's meet more often.

57) 일찍 돌아오세요.

   Please come back soon.

58) 이젠 작별하고 집에 돌아갈 시간이네요.

   It's time to say goodbye and go home.

II. Everyday English

59) 여러분 모두가 보고 싶을 겁니다.

    I shall miss all of you.

60) 다시 뵐 날을 학수고대합니다.

    I am looking forward to seeing you again.

2. Weather

Useful Expressions

1. 날씨 묻기

How will the weather be tomorrow?
What will the weather be like tomorrow?
What is the weather going to be like tomorrow?
How is it outside?
How's the weather today?
What's the weather forecast for today?

2. 좋은 날씨 궂은 날씨

It's a nice and warm day, isn't it?
It's a lovely day today, isn't it?
What a beautiful day!
I hope it stays like this.
I hope it will clear.
Nasty weather, isn't it?
It seems to be overcast today.
What mixed weather, now fine, then showery!

3. 비가 올 때

It's only a passing shower.
It's raining heavily outside.
It's likely to rain.
What if it pours this afternoon?
It is raining cats and dogs.
We'll have rain tomorrow.

II. Everyday English

4. 바람이 불 때

It is so windy!
It's windy today.
The wind is like a knife.
The wind has faded.
The wind is calming down.

5. 눈이 올 때

The snow is falling fast.
It often snows here.
It is snowing heavily.
It looks like snows.

6. 추울 때

It's a bit cold today.
It's the dead of winter.
We had a temperature of minus 10 this morning.
It's freezing (biting) cold, isn't it?
Cover/Wrap yourself up, please.

7. 더울 때

Terribly hot, isn't it?
It is burningly (blisteringly) hot.
It's as hot as hell.
I'm drenched with sweat.
I can't stand the summer weather.
I'm dying of the heat.
This heat wave is murder.

II. Everyday English

Speaking in English

1) 오늘 날씨가 어떻습니까?
   What is the weather like today?

2) 날씨가 무덥군요.
   It's hot and humid.

3) 대구의 여름은 언제나 이렇게 덥나요?
   Are summers always this hot in Daegu?

4) 네, 7, 8월은 푹푹 찌죠.
   Yes. July and August are roasting/boiling.

5) 지금 기온이 어떻게 돼요?
   What is the temperature now?

6) 아마 33도 가량 될 거예요.
   I'd say it's about 33 degrees.

7) 바깥 날씨가 어떻습니까?
   How is the weather out there?

8) 쌀쌀해요.
   It's chilly.

9) 비가 올 것 같나요?
   Do you think it might rain?

10) 오늘은 화창합니다.
    It is sunny today.

11) 오늘은 바람이 많이 붑니다.
    It is windy today.

II. Everyday English

12) 오늘은 안개가 끼었습니다.
    It is foggy today.

13) 가랑비가 내리기 시작하네요.
    It's beginning to sprinkle.

14) 비오는 날을 좋아하세요?
    Do you like rainy days?

15) 바깥기온이 영하로 떨어졌겠는데요.
    It must be below zero out there.

16) 일기예보는 오늘 밤이 어떨 거라고 합니까?
    What's the weather forecast for tonight?

17) 기상 캐스터는 오늘 밤 눈이 올 거라고 예보하더군요.
    The weatherman predicted snow tonight.

18) 당장이라도 눈이 내릴 것 같은데요.
    It looks like it's going to snow at any minute.

19) 그렇다면 출퇴근 시간엔 길이 막히겠는데요.
    That means the traffic will be terrible at rush hour.

20) 고향의 기후는 어떻습니까?
    What is the weather like in your hometown?

21) 이런 날씨 좋아하세요?
    Do you like this kind of weather?

22) 날씨가 참 좋죠?
    Isn't it a wonderful day?

23) 오늘은 날씨가 어떻습니까?
    How is the weather today?

II. Everyday English

24) 오늘은 날씨가 좋습니다.
The weather is nice today.

25) 어제는 날씨가 어떠했습니까?
What was the weather like yesterday?

26) 어제는 하루 종일 비가 왔습니다.
Yesterday it rained all day.

27) 내일은 날씨가 어떨까요?
What will the weather be like tomorrow?

28) 내일은 눈이 올 것입니다.
It's going to snow tomorrow.

29) 오늘은 날씨가 꽤 덥습니다.
It's quite hot today.

30) 오전 내내 구름이 끼었어요.
It's been cloudy all morning.

31) 지금 비가 오고 있습니까?
Is it raining now?

32) 오늘 오후에는 아마도 개일 것입니다.
It'll probably clear up this afternoon.

33) 날씨가 점점 더 더워지고 있습니다.
It is getting hotter and hotter.

34) 날씨가 어제보다 훨씬 더 덥습니다.
It is much hotter than it was yesterday.

35) 오늘이 여름의 첫 날입니다.
Today is the first day of summer.

II. Everyday English

36) 오늘은 몇 도 입니까?
    What's the temperature today?

37) 오늘 오후는 화씨 약 70도 입니다.
    It's about seventy degrees Fahrenheit this afternoon.

38) 오늘 저녁에는 시원한 미풍이 붑니다.
    There's a cool breeze this evening.

39) 저는 더운 날씨를 가장 좋아 합니다.
    I prefer hot weather.

40) 개인적으로, 저는 여름 날씨를 더 좋아합니다.
    Personally, I prefer summer weather.

41) 당신은 내일 비가 올 거라고 생각하십니까?
    Do you think it's going to rain tomorrow?

42) 저는 비가 올지 안 올지 모 르겠습니다.
    I don't know whether it will rain or not.

43) 진눈개비가 내린가요?
    Is it sleeting now?

44) 우박이 내린가요?
    Is it hailing now?

45) 이슬비가 내린가요?
    Is it drizzling?

46) 만약 내일 비가 오지 않으면 등산이나 갈까 합니다.
    If it doesn't rain tomorrow, I think I'll go mountain climbing.

47) 만약 내일 비가 오지 않으면 낚시나 갈까 합니다.
    If it doesn't rain tomorrow, I think I'll go fishing.

II. Everyday English

48) 광주 날씨가 마음에 드세요?

    Do you like the weather in Gwangju?

49) 예, 날씨가 매우 상쾌합니다.

    Yes, the weather is very nice.

50) 오늘의 날씨는 완벽합니다.

    The weather is perfect today.

3. Time & Date

Useful Expressions

1. 날짜를 물을 때

   What's the date today?
   What day of the month is it today?
   What's the occasion?
   What date is next Saturday?

2. 요일 · 월을 물을 때

   What day is it today?
   What day of the week is it today?
   What day does New Year's Day fall on next year?
   What month is this?

3. 요일 · 날짜에 답할 때

   It is July 30.
   It's Monday.
   It's Wednesday, August 1.
   Today is August 1st, 2015.

4. 시간을 물을 때

   What time is it now?
   Do you have the time?
   I wonder what time it is.

5. 시간을 답할 때

It's seven o'clock in the morning.
It's a quarter past ten.
It's four-thirty in the afternoon.
It's 10 minutes to nine.
It is about two o'clock.

6. 시작 시간 · 마감 시간을 물을 때

What time shall we start the meeting?
What time did you check-in?
What time does the program begin?
What time do you have the last train?
When does the cafe close?

7. 기한을 말할 때

Finish this work by the end of the week.
The contract lasts for three years.
This ticket is good for seven days.
You should come back in a few days.
I'll let you know by next Monday.

8. 소요 시간을 물을 때

How long does it take to get to your work?
How long does it take from LA to New York?
How long does the meeting last?
How long is the lunch break?

II. Everyday English

Speaking in English

1) 몇 시 입니까?

   What time is it?

2) 2시 입니다.

   It's two o'clock.

3) 2시 조금 지났습니다.

   It's a few minutes after two.

4) 내 시계는 빠르고 당신의 시계는 느립니다.

   My watch is fast and your watch is slow.

5) 실례합니다. 정확한 시간을 알려주실 수 있겠습니까?

   Excuse me. Can you tell me the correct time?

6) 저는 몇 시인지 모르겠습니다.

   I don't know what time it is.

7) 저는 벌써 4시가 되었다고는 생각하지 않습니다.

   I don't think it's four o'clock yet.

8) 약 3시 30분쯤 되었을 것입니다.

   It must be about three thirty.

9) 저는 매일 6시 전에 일어납니다.

   I get up before six o'clock every day.

10) 그 식당은 7시 45분까지는 열지 않습니다.

    The restaurant doesn't open until seven forty-five.

11) 내일 10시에 여기에 오시겠습니까?

    Will you be here at ten o'clock tomorrow?

II. Everyday English

12) 제 시간에 갈 수 있겠죠, 그렇지요?
    We'll be on time, won't we?

13) 그러기를 바랍니다.
    I hope so.

14) 오늘은 며칠입니까?
    What's the date today?

15) 오늘은 2018년 8월 1일입니다.
    Today is August 1st, 2018.

16) 당신은 언제 태어났습니까?
    When were you born?

17) 나는 1990년 11월 1일에 태어났습니다.
    I was born on November first, nineteen ninety.

18) 내 누이는 1998년에 태어났습니다.
    My sister was born in nineteen ninety-eight.

19) 나는 정확한 날짜는 모르겠습니다.
    I don't know the exact date.

20) 그 일을 다음 주까지는 끝내십시오.
    Finish the work by next week.

21) 이곳에서 5시까지 기다리고 계세요.
    Wait for me here until five o'clock.

22) 생태도시 순천에 대해서 무엇을 알고 있습니까?
    What do you know about the Ecological city, Suncheon?

23) 그것에 대해서는 아무 것도 모르고 있습니다.
    I don't know anything about that.

II. Everyday English

24) 점심시간은 얼마 동안이죠?
    How long is the lunch break?

25) 작년 4월 중에는 어디에 있었습니까?
    Where were you in April last year?

26) 그때 내가 어디에 있었는지 기억이 나지 않습니다.
    I don't remember where I was then.

27) 내년 이맘때는 어디에 계실 겁니까?
    Where will you be at this time next year?

28) 오늘은 무슨 요일입니까?
    What day is it today?

29) 오늘은 월요일입니다.
    It is Monday today.

30) 어제는 무슨 요일이었습니까?
    What day was yesterday?

31) 어제는 일요일이었습니다.
    Yesterday was Sunday.

32) 내일은 무슨 요일입니까?
    What day is tomorrow?

33) 다음 달은 몇 월입니까?
    What month is next month?

34) 나는 여러 주일 동안 입원해 있었습니다.
    I was in the hospital for several weeks.

35) 당신은 화요일에 어디 있었죠?
    Where were you on Tuesday?

II. Everyday English

36) 당신은 2월에 여기에 있었죠, 그렇죠?

   You were here in February, weren't you?

37) 당신 친구는 일주일 전에 여기 있었죠, 그렇죠?

   Your friend was here a week ago, wasn't he?

38) 그는 언제 돌아오리라 봅니까?

   When do you expect him back?

39) 10분 있으면 올 것입니다.

   He'll be back in ten minutes.

40) 내 시계가 2분 빠릅니다.

   My watch is two minutes fast.

41) 내 시계는 5분 정도 느립니다.

   My watch is about five minutes slow.

42) 내 시계는 7시 10분을 가리키고 있어요.

   My watch says seven ten.

43) 내 시계는 잘 맞아요.

   My watch keeps good time.

44) 내 시계는 하루에 10분 더 갑니다.

   My watch gains ten minutes a day.

45) 오늘이 무슨 날인데요? 오늘이 당신 생일 아닙니까.

   What's the occasion? It's your birthday, isn't it?

46) 수업시간에 늦지 않도록 해야 돼.

   Be sure to be in time for the class.

47) 시간에 꼭 맞춰야 해.

   Be sure to be on time.

II. Everyday English

48) 시간이 얼마나 걸린다고 생각하십니까?

   How long do you think it'll take?

49) 이젠 가야 할 시간이네요

   It's time to go now.

50) 저는 언제나 수업에 늦는 일이 없었어요.

   I was always punctual for class.

4. Emotion

Useful Expressions

1. 격려

Don't give in to it.
Pull yourself together.
Hang in there! / That's the way to go!
Let's cheer her up.
You'll get better soon.
I wish you a speedy recovery.

2. 동정

That's too bad.
Don't worry about it.
Keep your chin up.
It's not the end of the world.
Don't stop trying.
Try to forget the past.
Try not to focus on your past.

3. 만족할 때

We are pleased to win the championship.
I had a very pleasant experience there.
It's a nice job. I like it very much.
The negotiations were satisfactory.
If it's good enough for you, it's good enough for me.
This is a sufficient result.

4. 불만

Can you keep your voice down?
Don't you think you're being too rude?
I thought I told you to finish that up.
Don't blame it on me.
Who allowed you to do such a thing?
You're missing the point.
You expect too much from me.
Watch your tongue!

5. 기쁨

That's terrific (great/good).
I'm glad to hear that.
That's very good news.
I'm glad you could drop in.
I was delighted to hear the news of your success.
It's my pleasure to be of service to you.
I shall be delighted to come.

6. 슬픔

That's a shame.
What a pity!
I'm sorry to hear that.
What's the problem?
I'm sorry to have made you feel gloomy.
Cry your heart out!
Her tears are crocodile tears.

7. 분노

He's hot tempered. He's mad at you.
That infuriates/enrages me.
You look angry. Don't lose your temper.
You should be ashamed of yourself.
I can't figure out why he's so nervous.
Don't pull my leg.
I've never been so insulted.
It drives me crazy.
It's none of your business.

8. 두려움

I got so scared that I couldn't move.
I was scared to death.
The mere thought of it makes me shudder.
That movie gave me goose bumps.
I trembled (shivered) with horror from head to toe.
His story gave me the creeps.
Don't be a chicken.

9. 놀람

It's incredible.
That's news to me!
(What a) surprise!
It's amazing!
You're kidding!
I'm amazed that he accepted it.

II. Everyday English

Speaking in English

1) 자, 힘을 내. 너는 할 수 있어.
   Come on, you can do that.

2) 뭐든지 말씀만 해 보십시오. 다 있을 겁니다.
   You name it and I've got it.

3) 훌륭히 해냈어요.
   You did a good job.

4) 난 네가 자랑스럽다.
   I'm so proud of you.

5) 이길 수도 있지요. 가능성은 양쪽 다 똑같으니까.
   You might win. The odds are even/It is fifty fifty.

6) 당신은 틀림없이 해낼 수 있을 것이라고 믿어요.
   I bet you can make it.

7) 걱정할 것 하나도 없어요.
   You have nothing to worry about.

8) 부담스럽게 생각하지 마세요.
   Think nothing of it.

9) 기운 내! (용기를 내!)
   Cheer up!

10) 낙담하지 말아요.
    Don't be so sad.

11) 당신의 마음을 잘 알아요.
    I know how you feel.

II. Everyday English

12) 인생은 다 그런 거예요.
    Such is life!/That's life!

13) 그렇다면 더 더욱 좋지요.
    So much the better.

14) 누워서 떡먹기예요.
    It's a piece of cake.

15) 물론 말할 것도 없죠.
    Sure. That goes without saying.

16) 좀 더 힘내세요.
    You are almost there!

17) 머리를 쥐어짜내봐!
    Think harder!

18) 내가 보기에 너는 대성할 사람이야.
    You are the apple of my eye.

19) 그 얘긴 잊어버리세요. 그건 도저히 실현될 수 없는 계획이야.
    Your can forget it. It's only a pipe dream.

20) 모든 게 잘될 거예요.
    Everything will be fine.

21) 어려울 때는 저한테 오세요.
    Come to me if you are in any difficulty.

22) 당신 옆에서 고수할게요.
    I'll stick by you.

23) 내 문제와 비교하면 아무것도 아니에요.
    It's nothing compared to my problem.

II. Everyday English

24) 해보지 않고는 스스로의 능력을 알 수가 없지요.
You never know what you can do till you try.

25) 조만간에 그것을 알게 될 거예요.
You'll understand it sooner or later.

26) 남자답게 싫은 일도 참으세요.
Take your medicine like a man.

27) 필요한 건 용기만 조금 있으면 돼요. 그것이면 충분하다구요.
All it takes is a little courage. That's all there is to it.

28) 나중에는 그러길 잘했다고 하실 거예요.
In the long run, you'll be glad you did.

29) 음, 하지만 세상만사가 다 그런 거 아니겠어요?
Well, that's life, isn't it?

30) 소신껏 하세요.
Have it your own way.

31) 일단 요령만 익히면 어렵지 않아요.
It's not hard once you get the hang(knack) of it.

32) 진정하세요.
Calm down.

33) 자, 기운을 내세요.
Come on, snap out of it!

34) 당신도 그 요령을 알게 될거예요.
You will get the hang of it.

35) 뭐 그런 것 가지고 화를 내세요?
There's no reason to get so angry.

36) 당신의 답에 제가 만족할 겁니다.
    Whatever your answer is, I will be satisfied.

37) 보기보다 어렵지 않아요.
    It is not as difficult as it looks.

38) 세상만사가 다 그렇고 그런것.
    That's the way the cookie crumbles.

39) 없는 것보다는 낫잖아요.
    It's better than nothing.

40) 당신은 결코 실패할 리 없어요.
    It is impossible to associate failure with you.

41) 그건 당신한테 딱 들어맞아요.
    That's just your pace.

42) 걱정 말고 말해요.
    Come out and say it.

43) 그런 사소한 일로 상심하지 마세요.
    Please don't brood over such a trivial matter.

44) 저는 일에 많이 시달리고 있어요.
    I'm under a lot of pressure at work.

45) 한 사람이 하기엔 일이 너무 벅차요.
    There's just too much work for one person.

46) 곧 시달림에서 벗어났으면 좋겠군요.
    Well, I hope the pressure is off you soon.

47) 그녀는 신경질 나서 죽을지 경에 있어요.
    She's a nervous wreck.

II. Everyday English

48) 폐를 끼치고 싶지 않은데

   I hope I'm not imposing.

49) 오늘 제가 제 정신이 아니군요.

   I'm not feeling myself today.

50. 놀리시는 겁니까?

   Are you pulling my leg?

5. Telephone

Useful Expressions

1. 전화 발신

May I speak to Jessica, please?
Is Mr. Johnson in?
I'd like to speak to Mrs. Cook, please.
Is this the Mr. Park's residence?
Is Mr. Lee available?

2. 전화 수신

This is Kate speaking.
GM Trading Company. May I help you?
Who's calling, please?
Who would you like to speak to?
Can I have your name, please?

3. 용건 문답

What is this call regarding?
What are you calling about?
Can I ask what this call is about?
I'd like to make an appointment with you tomorrow. I just called to say hello.
I have some important business to talk about.
I am returning his call.

4. 부재중

He's not in.
I'm sorry, but he's not at his desk right now.
He just left for home.
He just stepped out for a moment.
He's on a business trip in Seoul all this week.
Sorry, but he is out to lunch.
May I take your message?
He'll be back in about 30 minutes.
You can reach him by calling 343-2799.
Call me between two and three.

5. 기다림

Can you hold, please?
Hold on a second. Please don't hang up.
Just one moment. I'll put you through.
Just a minute. I will connect you with her office.
I'm sorry, but his line is busy at the moment.
Can I call you right back?

6. 약속

How can I get in touch with you?
Would you mind giving me a call?
What time will you be home tomorrow?
When is the best time to reach you?
Can I see you at seven on Saturday?
Is May 5th a good date?

7. 국제 전화

Can I call overseas from this phone?
I'd like to make an international call to Canada.
Would you connect me with an operator in LA?
I'll put you through to the international operator.
The area code is 062, and the number is 232-4321.
Could you tell me the length and the charge of the call?
Tom wants a collect call from New York.

8. 교환을 통한 전화

Please hang up and wait.
Your call won't take long, hang on a moment.
It's ringing but no one is answering.
Your party doesn't answer.
Your party is on the line.
The line is connected.
Mr. Kate is on the line. Go ahead, please.
You have an overseas collect call from US.
Will you accept the charges?

9. 공중전화

Do you have a pay phone around here?
I'm calling from a public phone.
Lift the receiver, deposit the coin and dial.
Deposit 80 cents, please.

II. Everyday English

Speaking in English

1) 당신에게 전화 왔습니다.

   You're wanted on the telephone.

2) 존, 당신 전화인데요.

   John, it's for you.

3) 2번 전화 받으시겠어요.

   Can you take a call on line two?

4) 전화 온 것 있어요?

   Did anyone call?

5) 내가 밖에 있는 동안 전화 온 거 있었나요?

   Were there any calls for me while I was out?

6) 다른 전화로 받지요.

   I'll use the other phone (line).

7) 그 사람과 연결시켜 주세요.

   Put him through.

8) 샘 좀 바꿔 주시겠어요.

   Can you put me through to Sam?

9) 그녀가 언제쯤 돌아(들어) 올 것 같아요?

   When do you expect her back (in)?

10) 메시지를 남기시겠습니까?

    Would you like to leave a message?

11) 좀 더 크게 말씀해 주시겠어요?

    Would you speak up, please?

II. Everyday English

12) 그녀는 (통화를 끝내고) 전화를 끊었어요.

    She hung up.

13) 존의 전화번호를 아세요?

    Do you have John's number?

14) 아무도 전화를 안 받네요.

    There is no answer.

15) 전화번호를 다시 한번 말씀 해 주세요.

    Would you repeat that number?

16) 교환에게 걸려면 몇 번을 걸어야 합니까?

    What number should I dial to get the operator?

17) 장거리 전화를 걸고 싶습니다.

    I want to make a long distance call.

18) 당신은 전화를 틀림없이 잘못 거셨습니다.

    You must have dialed the wrong number.

19) 저는 전화를 제대로 걸었지만 아무도 받지 않았습니다.

    I dialed the right number, but nobody answered.

20) 전화가 울리고 있습니다. 전화 좀 받아 주시겠습니까?

    The telephone is ringing. Would you answer it, please?

21) 누구십니까? 당신 목소리를 알 수가 없는데요.

    Who is this? I don't recognize your voice.

22) 광주 252국에 4093번입니까?

    Is this Gwangju 252-4093?

23) 이제 전화를 끊어야 하겠습니다.

    I have to hang up now.

II. Everyday English

24) 내일 언젠가 다시 전화해주시겠습니까?
    Would you mind calling back sometime tomorrow?

25) 돌리신 321-1234 번호는 끊겼습니다.
    The number you have reached 321-1234 has been disconnected.

26) 한국 서울로 수신자 요금부담 전화를 좀 하고 싶은데요.
    I'd like to make a collect call to Seoul, Korea.

27) 웨인 씨의 수신자부담 전화입니다. 전화요금을 부담하시겠습니까?
    There's a collect call from Mr. Wayne. Will you accept the charge?

28) 통화를 다 하셨나요?
    Are you through with your call?

29) 통화중 신호만 계속 들립니다.
    It keeps getting a busy signal.

30) 그녀의 전화는 항상 통화중 이어요.
    Her line is always busy.

31) 제가 당신에게 어떻게 하면 연락할 수 있나요?
    How can I get in touch with you?

32) 555-1212로 전화하시면 제게 연락됩니다.
    You can reach me by calling 555-1212.

33) 이 번호로 항상 연락이 되나요?
    Are you at this number all the time?

34) 다섯 시 이후에는 567-8000 으로 전화하시면 됩니다.
    You can reach me at 567- 8000 after five.

35) 지금 몹시 급한 일에 매여 계신데요.
    He's tied up at the moment.

II. Everyday English

36) 미안합니다만 지금 회의 중 이신데요. 제가 도와 드릴까요?
    I'm sorry he's in a conference now. May I help you with something?

37) 미안합니다. 구내전화를 잘못 거셨습니다.
    I'm sorry, you have the wrong extension.

38) 이 전화를 그의 사무실로 돌려 주시겠습니까?
    Will you transfer this call to his office?

39) 네, 하지만 제가 전화를 돌려 드리는 동안 끊지 말고 기다리십시오.
    Yes, but please hold while I transfer your call.

40) 그 사람에게로 전화를 돌려 주시겠습니까?
    Can you switch over to his extension?

41) 미안합니다만 안 됩니다. 그에게 직접 전화를 하셔야 됩니다.
    No, I'm sorry. You'll have to call him directly.

42) 잠시만 기다려 주십시오. 불러서 찾아보겠습니다.
    One moment, please. I'll page him.

43) 죄송합니다만, 방금 나가셨습니다.
    I'm sorry, but he has just stepped out.

44) 통화중이십니다.
    He's on another line.

45) 죄송합니다만 지금 전화 받고 계십니다. 기다리시겠습니까?
    I'm sorry, he's on the phone. Will you hold?

46) 자리에 계신지 알아보겠습니다.
    I'll see if he's in.

47) 그분은 퇴근하셨습니다.
    He just left for the day.

II. Everyday English

48) 그분은 여름휴가를 떠났습니다.
   He's gone for the summer.

49) 전화를 거시도록 할까요?
   Shall I have him return the call?

50) (그가 전화 하셨다기에) 답례 전화를 드리는 것입니다.
   I'm returning his call.

51) 내일 다시 전화하지요.
   I'll call back tomorrow.

52) 좋습니다. 다시 전화하신다고 전해 드리죠.
   O.K. I'll tell him you'll call again.

53) 미스터 웨인, 전화왔습니다.
   Mr. Wayne, there's a call for you.

54) 급한 일이라고 하시는데요.
   He says it's urgent.

55) 내 사무실에서 받지요.
   I'll take it in my office.

56) 전하실 말씀이 있습니까?
   Would you care to leave a message?

57) 메시지를 남기시겠어요?
   Would you like to leave a message?

58) 무슨 일로 전화하셨습니까?
   What's this regarding?

59) 알겠습니다. 전화하셨다고 전해 드리지요.
   All right. I'll tell him you called.

60) 이 건물 안에 공중전화가 있습니까?
   Is there a public telephone in this building?

II. Everyday English

6. Hobbies

Useful Expressions

1. 취미

What are your hobbies?
What do you do in your free time?
I enjoy reading fantasy novels.
I love to collect movie posters.
I'm taking guitar lessons as a hobby.
Tastes differ.
Are you interested in Korean paintings?
We have many hobbies in common.
It doesn't suit my tastes.
I have no particular hobbies.
We have quite different tastes.

2. 야외 활동

I am going on vacation next week.
I'd like to travel to Busan by train.
I'll pack my bags tonight.
We went sightseeing and took some pictures.
I want to buy a souvenir for my friend.
My family often goes hiking in the mountains.
We finally reached the top of the mountain.
We looked for a place to put up a tent.

3. 오락

What's on TV?
Turn on the radio, will you?
This radio has a fine tone.
Yesterday I bought a portable TV set.
Does it have a clear picture?
I'd like to have my TV set fixed.
What's the trouble?
The picture tube is worn out.
How's your TV set working?

4. 영화 · 연극

Where can I buy tickets?
What's playing at the National Theater?
I'd like two tickets for tonight's performance.
Do you have any seats in a high balcony?
I'd like a general admission seat, please.
Is there a cover charge?
Who starred in the movie?
It's dubbed in Korean.

5. 음 악

What kind of music do you listen to?
I have no ear for music.
I like almost every kind of music.
I'm crazy about classical music.
Do you play any musical instrument?
He's good at singing.

II. Everyday English

Speaking in English

1) 취미가 뭡니까?
   What's your hobby?

2) 낚시를 즐겨합니다.
   I enjoy fishing.

3) 제 취미는 우표수집입니다.
   My hobby is collecting stamps.

4) 많이 수집하셨어요?
   Do you have a big collection?

5) 여가를 어떻게 보내세요?
   What do you do for relaxation?

6) 여가에는 무엇을 하나요?
   What do you do in your spare time?

7) 우편수집에 관심이 있습니까?
   Are you interested in collecting stamps?

8) 좋아하는 팝송이 무엇입니까?
   What's your favorite pop song?

9) 야구경기 관람을 즐겨 하십니까?
   Do you enjoy watching the baseball game?

10) 악기 다룰 줄 아세요?
    Do you play any musical instruments?

11) 그 노래 기타로 연주할 줄 아세요?
    Do you know how to play any songs on the guitar?

12) 그 음악은 나의 취향에 맞지 않아요.
   That music is not to my taste.

13) 저는 가수 마이클 잭슨을 아주 좋아해요.
   I'm crazy about Michael Jackson, a singer.

14) 텔레비전에 뭐가 방영되고 있어요?
   What's on TV?

15) 어느 프로그램을 가장 좋아 합니까?
   Which program do you enjoy the most?

16) 토크쇼를 가장 좋아합니다.
   I enjoy talk shows the most.

17) 당신 특기가 뭐예요?
   What is your specialty?

18) 어떤 종류의 음악을 좋아하세요?
   What's your favorite kind of music?

19) 무슨 레코드를 듣고 싶어요?
   What record would you like to hear?

20) 그 노래를 들으니 그리운 옛 추억이 되살아나는군요.
   That song brings back old memories.

21) 그녀는 음악에 조예가 깊습니다.
   She has an ear for music.

22) 그녀는 그림을 감상할 줄 아는 심미안이 있어요.
   She has an eye for paintings.

23) 나는 (체질적으로) 춤추는 것을 좋아하지 않아요.
   I don't go in for dancing.

II. Everyday English

24) 나는 손에 집히는 대로 다 읽어요.

   I read everything I can get my hands on.

25) 그 책 다 읽었어요?

   Are you through with the book?

26) 나는 이렇게 감동적인 책을 읽어 본 적이 없어요.

   I've never read a more stirring story.

27) 이 책은 내 사고방식에 영향을 주었습니다.

   This book has affected my thinking.

28) 이 그림이 진본인지를 구별 하기가 힘들군요.

   It's hard to tell if this picture is an original.

29) 남편은 정원 가꾸기를 무척 좋아했었죠.

   My husband used to be very fond of gardening.

30) 매일 일기를 씁니까?

   Do you keep a diary every day?

31) 얼마나 자주 낚시를 가십니까?

   How often do you go fishing?

32) 이번 일요일에 함께 갈까요?

   Shall we go together this Sunday?

33) 시간을 보내기 위해 때때로 전자 오락게임을 해요.

   I sometimes play video games to kill time.

34) 취미삼아 하는 건가요, 생계 수단인가요?

   Do you do that for a hobby or for a living?

35) 빗속을 거닐기를 좋아하세요?

   Do you like walking in the rain?

II. Everyday English

36) 동전 수집은 재미있으나, 값진 주화를 구하기는 하늘의 별 따기에요.
    Coin collecting is interesting, but you find a valuable coin only once in a blue moon.

37) 우리 제비뽑기로 합시다.
    Let's draw lots.

38) 동전을 던져서 결정합시다.
    Let's flip for it.

39) 편을 가릅시다.
    Let's make two teams.

40) 수수께끼 하나 물어볼까?
    Let me ask you a riddle.

41) 스무고개를 하자.
    Let's play 20 questions.

42) 숨바꼭질하자.
    Let's play hide and seek.

43) 누구 차례인가요?
    Whose turn is it?

44) 먼저 패부터 떼지 그래.
    Cut the cards first.

45) 넌 패가 좋구나. (화투, 트럼프)
    You have a good hand of cards.

46) 잠깐만요, 제 목소리 좀 가다 듣고요.
    Wait a minute, I should clear my throat first.

47) 그녀는 노래를 잘한다.

II. Everyday English

She sings like a bird.

48) 나는 음치예요.
I can't carry a tune.

49) 매우 즐거웠어요.
I was tickled to death.

50) 골프에 관한 것이라면 자네도 그에게 못 당할걸.
When it comes to golf, you can't beat him.

51) 우리 프로그램이 매일 아침 방송됩니다.
Our show is aired every morning.

52) 오늘 프로가 뭐죠?
What's on today?

53) 그건 어떻게 켜는 겁니까?
How do I turn it on?

54) 채널 9에서는 뭘 하죠?
What's on Channel 9?

55) 신문에 텔레비전 프로그램에 대해 어떻게 나와 있어요?
What does the newspaper say about the TV program?

56) 오늘밤 채널 9에서 좋은 영화를 방영하는군요.
There's a good movie on Channel 9 tonight.

57) 내가 좋아하는 연속극을 안 놓치고 싶어요.
I don't want to miss my favorite soap opera.

58) 한국 TV 연속극들은 대개 눈물만 짜게 해요.
Most Korean TV series are tear-jerkers.

II. Everyday English

59) 우리 TV가 잘 안 나와요.
I don't get a good picture on my TV set.

60) 화면의 초점이 맞지 않습니다.
The picture is out of focus.

7. Invitation & Visit

Useful Expressions

1. 초대

How about having dinner with me tomorrow?
Let me treat you to dinner.
Can you come over to my place for dinner?
I'd like to invite you to dinner tomorrow.
We request the honor (pleasure) of your company.
Could you join the party?
Any day will be fine. You decide when.
Thank you, I'd be glad to come.
It's very kind of you to invite me.
I'd love to, but I won't be able to come.
I'm sorry, but I have another appointment.
Can I get a rain check, please?

2. 방문

Is this Mr. Johnson's home(residence)?
Would you mind if I take a look around your house?
(Giving a present) Here's a little something for you.
It looks very good and juicy. Wow, it's very delicious.
May I have some more potatoes?
Thank you, but I've had more than enough.
I'll take my coffee black.
I'm afraid I'd better be leaving.
Thank you so much for everything. I really enjoyed it.

3. 접대

Thank you for coming. We've been expecting you.
Did you have trouble finding our house?
(Receiving the present) Oh, how nice! I like it.
Take off your jacket and make yourself at home.
Should I show you around our house?
Please help yourself. Take it before it gets cold.
How does the steak taste?
Would you like some more?
Let me know if you need anything.
Which would you prefer, tea or coffee?
Why don't you stay longer?
I'm very happy you enjoyed yourself.
Let me follow you to the door.
Please come and see us again sometime.
I'll drive you home in my car.

4. 파티

We want to give you a welcome party.
Please, bring your wife, too.
That would be wonderful.
When are you having the party?
Should I dress up for the party?
Would you care for a drink?
Let's toast to the bride and groom!
Let's drink to his success.

Ⅱ. Everyday English

Speaking in English

1) 저녁식사에 선생님을 초대하고 싶습니다.
   I'd like to invite you to have dinner with us.

2) 내일 우리와 함께 저녁이나 하러 오시지요.
   Won't you come and have dinner with us tomorrow?

3) 와 주셔서 고마워요
   I'm glad you could come.

4) 초대해 주셔서 감사합니다.
   Thank you for the invitation.

5) 들어오시죠?
   Won't you come in?

6) 신을 신고 들어오세요.
   Please come in with your shoes on.

7) 집이 참 좋군요.
   You have a nice house.

8) 편히 쉬세요.
   Make yourself at home.

9) 오길 잘 했군요.
   I'm glad I came.

10) 코트를 벗어 주시겠습니까?
    May I take your coat?

11) 집안을 안내해 드리죠. 여기가 거실입니다.
    I'll show you around our home. This is our living room.

II. Everyday English

12) 과자 좀 드시죠.
　　Please help yourself to the cookies.

13) 존스 씨를 좀 뵙고 싶습니다.
　　I'd like to see Mr. Jones for a moment.

14) 잠깐만 기다려 주세요.
　　Please wait a moment.

15) 죄송하지만 존스 씨는 외출 중입니다.
　　I'm sorry. Mr. Jones is out.

16) 존스 씨는 언제 돌아오십니까?
　　When is Mr. Jones expected back?

17) 메모를 남기시겠습니까?
　　Will you leave a message?

18) 오늘밤에 찾아 뵈도 되겠습니까?
　　May I call on you tonight?

19) 제가 몇 시에 올까요?
　　What time shall I come?

20) 이젠 가야 되겠습니다.
　　I'm afraid I have to go now.

21) 멋진 파티였어요.
　　It was a lovely party.

22) 감사합니다만, 이제 가야 할 것 같아요.
　　Thank you very much, but I guess I'd better go.

23) 실례해요. 자리를 뜨고 싶군요.
　　Please excuse me I'd like to leave.

II. Everyday English

24) 조만 간에 또 놀러 오세요.
   Please come again and see us sometime.

25) 와 주셔서 참 즐거웠습니다.
   We really enjoyed your company.

26) 그럼, 다음 기회에 모일 수 있겠죠.
   Well, then, perhaps we can get together another time.

27) 조만간에 다시 한자리 만듭시다.
   Let's get together soon.

28) 당신의 누이에게 안부 좀 전해 주십시오.
   Please give my best regards to your sister.

29) 아무쪼록 가족들에게 안부 부탁합니다.
   Give my regards to your family.

30) 존슨에게 안부 전해 주세요.
   Give my love to Johnson.

31) 좀 더 계시다 가시면 안 돼요?
   Can't you stay a little longer?

32) 지금 가신다는 말입니까?
   Do you mean you're going now?

33) 그렇게 서둘러 떠나지 마세요.
   Please don't be in such a hurry.

34) 계시다가 저녁 드시고 가시지 그러세요.
   Would you like to stay for dinner?

35) 저녁 드시고 가시지 않으시겠어요?
   Won't you stay for dinner?

II. Everyday English

36) 오늘 밤 재미있었어요?

    Did you have fun tonight?

37) 오늘 즐거우셨어요?

    Did you have a good time today?

38) 다시 만날 수 있을까요?

    Can we meet again?

39) 또 오세요.

    Come again.

40) 제가 바래다 드릴까요? (자동차로)

    Can I give you a lift?

41) 가봐야 하는 것 아닌가?

    Don't you think you'd better go?

42) 조금 더 계실 순 없나요?

    Can't you stay a little longer?

43) 또 와 주세요.

    Please come and see us again.

44) 오늘 밤에 한잔하는 게 어때요?

    How about a drink tonight?

45) 나는 술에 강합니다.

    I'm a heavy drinker.

46) 술은 한 방울도 입에 대지 않습니다.

    I don't drink a drop of alcohol.

47) 당신이 내는 건가요?

    Is it your treat?

II. Everyday English

48) 네, 제가 한잔 사는 겁니다.
    Yep. I'll buy you a drink.

49) 이 근처에 싱글들이 주로 가는 바아가 있나요?
    Is there a single's bar around here?

50) 네, 한 곳이 있는데 음악도 좋아요.
    Yes. There is one with excellent music.

51) 거기가 단골집인가요?
    Is it your hangout?

52) 각자 부담하도록 합시다.
    Let's split the bill.

53) 괜찮습니다. 제가 내지요.
    That's okay. It's my treat.

54) 오, 안 돼요. 당신이 혼자 내면 안 돼요.
    Oh, no. I can't let you do that.

55) 음, 이 맥주 아주 끝내 주는군요.
    Mmm, this beer hits the spot.

56) 더운 날에는 찬 맥주보다 더 좋은 것이 없다니까요.
    I know there is nothing like a cold beer on a hot day.

57) 푹 쉬는 데는 이보다 더 좋은 방법이 없지요.
    No better way to relax.

58) 점점 술기가 올라오는군요.
    I think I'm getting drunk.

59) 저는 정신이 말짱한 걸요.
    I'm completely sober.

II. Everyday English

60) 어젯밤에 꽤 취했어요.
   I got pretty drunk last night.

8. Opinions

Useful Expressions

1. 찬성할 때

I agree with the plan.
I agree with you on that.
That's an excellent idea.
I'm for it.
I'm all for it.
I'm in favor of that.
That's exactly what I was going to say.
I'm of the same opinion as you.
I couldn't agree more.
I can go along with you on that point.
You've got a point there.
There's something in what you say.
He nodded his head.

2. 대답을 보류할 때

I would have to think about it again.
Let me think about it.
Well, I'll think about it.
I'd rather not say right now.
I'm not sure whether I can agree.
That doesn't make sense to me.
I'll think about it and let you know my views tomorrow.

3. 반대할 때

I'm against him.
I don't think so.
I'm afraid you might be mistaken.
I can't go along with you on that.
I don't think it's a good idea.
I'm not so sure about that.
It's hard to say in a nutshell.
I'm afraid my opinion is a little different.
I have different ideas about it.
I wish I could agree with you.
It's out of the question.
I'm absolutely against that.
He left with a shake of his head.
She simply laughed off his proposal.

4. 불확실 할 때

That may be, but …….
You have a point, but …….
I suppose you're right, but …….
I respect your opinion, but …….
I appreciate your point of view, but …….
I agree with you to a certain degree, but …….
I may be wrong, but …….
I understand what you are saying, but …….
Oh, sorry, I was mixed up.
I was confused.

II. Everyday English

Speaking in English

1) 이걸 어떻게 하면 될까요?
   What should I do with this?

2) 이걸 어떻다고 생각하세요.
   What do you think about this?

3) 새로 산 내 차는 어떤 것 같아요?
   What do you think of my new car?

4) 그게 무슨 말이죠? (무슨 의미로 한 말이죠?)
   What do you mean by that?

5) 무슨 말을 하려는 거죠?
   What would you like to say?

6) 당신이 만일 내 처지라면 어떻게 하겠어요?
   What would you do if you were in my place?

7) 내게 설명 좀 해 주시겠어요?
   Can you fill me in?

8) 이런 상황에 대하여 조언이 필요합니다.
   I need some feedback on this situation.

9) 뭐라고요? (다시 한 번 말씀해 주시겠어요?)
   Pardon me? / Excuse me?

10) 그게 사실인가요?
    Is it true? / Is that right?

11) 그게 그런 건가요?
    Is that so?

II. Everyday English

12) 꼭 그렇지는 않아요.
    Not really.

13) 제가 한 말씀 드리겠습니다.
    Let me tell you something.

14) 잠시 한 말씀 드리겠어요.
    Give me the chance to explain.

15) 좋아요. 그럼 이렇게 하죠. (제가 뭔가를 말씀드리겠어요.)
    O.K. I'll tell you what.

16) 그게 전부입니다. 바로 그겁니다.
    That's it.

17) 정말 모르겠는데요.
    I don't have the slightest idea.

18) 자, 이제 어떡하면 되겠습니까?
    Now, what am I going to do?

19) 단도직입적으로 질문을 해도 괜찮겠습니까?
    Do you mind if I ask you some direct questions?

20) 제가 무엇을 했으면 합니까?
    What do you want me to do?

21) 공통점이 뭔가요?
    What do you have in common?

22) 하려는 말이 뭐죠?
    What do you have in mind?

23) 어떻게 뾰족한 수가 없을까요?
    Isn't there any way out?

II. Everyday English

24) 제때에 갈 수 있겠어요?
    Can you make it on time?

25) 누가 그 얘기를 하던가요?
    Who told you about that?

26) 신의 이름으로 맹세합니까?
    Do you swear in the name of God?

27) 이만하면 괜찮아 보입니까?
    Do I look all right?

28) 이건 어딘가 잘못되어 있는 것 같지 않아요?
    Maybe something is wrong?/Isn't this topsy-turvy?

29) 제가 싫다고 하면 어떻게 되는 거죠?
    What if I say no?

30) 그 사람은 자기가 해야 할 일을 알고 있나요?
    Does he know what to do?

31) 정말 모른단 말인가요?
    You mean you don't know?

32) 제 작품이 (제가 한 일이) 마음에 드세요?
    Are you happy with my work?

33) 내가 한 말 알아들었나요?
    Do you get me? (Get it?)

34) 의미가 통합니까? (말이 되나요?)
    Does it make sense?

35) 그건 식은 죽 먹기예요.
    It's a piece of cake!

36) 그 이야기를 들으니까 뭐가 떠오릅니까?
What does the story remind you of?

37) 당신은 어느 쪽 편입니까?
Which side are you on?

38) 모르시겠어요? (포기하시는 건가요?)
Are you going to give up?

39) 진정인가요, 아니면 농담인가요?
Are you serious or joking?

40) 한 몫 끼지 않을래요?
Why don't you take part?

41) 그게 뭐가 그리 좋아요?
What's so good about it?

42) 이게 정말 그럴까요?
Can this be true?

43) 좋은 생각이 떠오르세요?
Can you come up with an idea?

44) 우리들 중 누가 더 예쁘다고 생각하세요?
Which of us do you think is prettier?

45) 그렇게 생각하지만, 왜요?
I think so. Why?

46) 당신은 어떻게 생각하십니까? 그것이 옳습니까?
What do you think? Is that right?

47) 물론이지요. 그것에 대해서는 당신이 절대적으로 옳습니다.
Certainly. You're absolutely right about that.

II. Everyday English

48) 제 견해로는, 그것은 훌륭한 생각입니다.
In my opinion, that's an excellent idea.

49) 당신의 솔직한 의견을 알려 주십시오.
Please give me your frank opinion.

50) 물론 저는 당신의 의견이 어떤지 알고 싶습니다.
Of course I want to know what your opinion is.

51) 당신은 당신 견해를 갖고 있고, 저는 제 견해를 갖고 있습니다.
You have your point of view, and I have mine.

52) 당신은 제가 하는 것과는 다른 방식으로 그것에 접근하고 있습니다.
You approach it in a different way than I do.

53) 저는 당신과 논쟁하진 않겠습니다만, 당신이 부당하다고 생각합니다.
I won't argue with you, but I think you're being unfair.

54) 그것은 너그러운 견해입니다.
That's a liberal point of view.

55) 제가 어떤 대안을 가지고 있습니까? (제가 어떻게 해야죠?)
What alternatives do I have?

56) 모든 것에는 항상 양면이 있습니다.
There are always two sides to everything.

57) 우리는 이것에 대해 반대 의견을 가지고 있습니다.
We have opposite views on this.

58) 당신은 어떤 주장을 하시려 합니까?
What point are you trying to make?

59) 우리의 견해는 결국 아주 다른 것은 아닙니다.
Our views are not so far apart, after all.

II. Everyday English

60) 우리는 우리의 차이를 해결 할 수 있어야 합니다.
We should be able to resolve our differences.

9. Health

Useful Expressions

1. 건강 상태

How do you keep yourself fit?
What do you do to stay healthy?
What do you do to keep in shape?
I'm in the best condition.
I'm in a fairly good shape.
These days I feel pretty good.
Recently, I've had a big appetite.
My health is not so good.
I'm in poor shape.
I have suddenly lost weight.
I feel worse than usual.
I feel tired all the time.
I can't get to sleep. I'm suffering from insomnia.

2. 운동과 다이어트

What kind of exercises do you like?
Are you still keeping up with your morning exercise?
These days, I've been jogging fairly regularly.
Jogging does you good.
Have you ever gone on a diet?
I'm on a diet, I'm getting too fat.
I'm trying to watch my waist line.
You should resolve to lose weight.

3. 체중

He has lost 10 pounds.
You're underweight.
You've lost a little weight, haven't you?
I've slimmed down by three pounds.
I'm trying to make my waist slimmer.
I'm getting too fat.
I think I've gained weight.
I have put on at least 5 pounds.
You're overweight.
I've gained a bit of weight through lack of exercise.

4. 음식과 음료

What is your favorite food?
I like pork better than chicken.
I like grilled fish.
I have a sweet tooth.
I don't like greasy food.
I'm not picky about what I eat.
I'm not so particular about what I eat.
I prefer black tea to green tea.
Tea calms my nerves.
He's a connoisseur or an expert of tea.
I always start out the morning with a cup of coffee.
I like strong (weak) coffee.
I drink my coffee with cream and sugar.
I have three cups of coffee a day.

II. Everyday English

Speaking in English

1) 나는 건강합니다.
   I'm in good health.

2) 저는 완전히 지쳤어요.
   I'm worn out.

3) 나는 다이어트 중입니다.
   I'm on a diet.

4) 나는 체중이 줄었어요.
   I've been losing weight.

5) 난 5파운드나 빠졌다고요, 알아보겠어요?
   I've lost five pounds. Can you tell?

6) 그 사람 몸 컨디션이 좀 나빠요. (저기압이에요.)
   He's somewhat under the weather.

7) 전 오늘 몸이 좀 불편해요.
   I'm a little out of shape today.

8) 나는 속이 메스꺼워요.
   I feel sick to my stomach.

9) 토할 것 같아요.
   I think I'm going to throw up.

10) 열이 좀 있어요.
    I have a slight fever.

11) 암만해도 감기에 걸린 것 같아요.
    I seem to be coming down with a cold.

12) 저는 감기 증세가 좀 있습니다.
   I have a touch of the flu.

13) 당신은 감기 걸린 목소리군요.
   You sound like you've got a cold.

14) 나는 독감에 전염됐어요.
   I came down with the flu.

15) 아, 머리가 아파 죽겠어요.
   Oh, my head is killing me.

16) 머리가 띵해요.
   I have a dull headache.

17) 다리에 쥐가 났어요.
   I've got a cramp in my leg.

18) 목이 쉬었어요.
   My voice is hoarse.

19) 나는 기진맥진이에요.
   I feel run down.

20) 독감이 많이 유행하고 있어요.
   There's a lot of flu going around.

21) 지독하게 아프단 말이에요.
   They hurt like mad.

22) 귀가 멍멍해요.
   My ears are ringing.

23) 현기증이 나서 나는 기절할 뻔 했어요.
   I felt dizzy and almost fainted.

II. Everyday English

24) 나는 갑자기 식은땀을 흘렸어요.
   I broke out in a cold sweat.

25) 콧물이 흘러요.
   My nose is running.

26) 배탈이 났어요.
   I've got the runs.

27) 먹은 것 때문에 설사가 나요.
   I have loose bowels due to what I've eaten.

28) 그는 귀가 어두워요.
   He's hard of hearing.

29) 건망증이 심해지는 것 같아요.
   I think I'm losing my mind.

30) 나는 단 것을 되도록 안 먹고 있어요.
   I'm cutting down on sweets.

31) 그는 미끄러져서 발목을 삐었어요.
   He slipped and fell and sprained his ankle.

32) 어디에 걸려 넘어지셨어요?
   What did you trip over?

33) 아얏! 바늘에 찔렸어요.
   Ouch! I pricked myself with the needle.

34) 아, 가시가 박혔군요.
   Oh, you've got a splint.

35) 내 눈에 뭔가 들어갔어요.
   I've got something in my eyes.

36) 내 발가락이 동상에 걸렸어요.
   I got my toes injured because of the cold.

37) 병원에 가서 진찰을 받아 봐야겠어요.
   I have to go see the doctor.

38) 면도하다가 베었어요.
   I cut myself shaving.

39) 그는 몸에 큰 흉터가 있어요.
   He has a big scar on his body.

40) 의사한테 가보지 그래요?
   Why don't you go and see the doctor?

41) 오늘은 기분이 좀 어떻습니까?
   How are you feeling today?

42) 오늘 아침에는 썩 좋지 않습니다.
   I don't feel very well this morning.

43) 어제는 아팠지만, 오늘은 더 나아졌습니다.
   I was sick yesterday, but I'm better today.

44) 열은 사라졌지만, 아직 기침이 납니다.
   My fever is gone, but I still have a cough.

45) 내 형은 두통이 심합니다.
   My brother has a bad headache.

46) 당신의 어느 쪽 팔이 아픕니까?
   Which of your arms is sore?

47) 제 오른쪽 팔이 아픕니다. 바로 여기가 아픕니다.
   My right arm hurts. It hurts right here.

II. Everyday English

48) 무슨 일입니까?

    What's the matter with you?

49) 등에 통증이 있습니다.

    I've got a pain in my back.

50) 어느 발이 아픕니까? 왼쪽 발입니까?

    Which foot hurts? Is it the left one?

51) 당신 다리는 어떻게 하다가 부러졌습니까?

    How did you break your leg?

52) 계단에서 미끄러져 넘어졌습니다. 다리가 부러졌지요.

    I slipped on the stairs and fell down. I broke my leg.

53) 당신 오른 쪽 손이 부었군요. 아픕니까?

    Your right hand is swollen. Does it hurt?

54) 피가 나네요. 그 상처에 대해 의사 선생님을 찾아가는게 좋겠습니다.

    It's bleeding. You'd better go see a doctor about that cut.

55) 당신이 곧 좋아지기를 바랍니다.

    I hope you'll be well soon.

56) 저는 어제 건강 진단을 받으러 의사를 만나러 갔습니다.

    I went to see my doctor for a check-up yesterday.

57) 의사는 내가 약간 비만이라는 것을 발견했습니다.

    The doctor discovered that I'm a little overweight.

58) 그는 나의 가슴 엑스레이를 찍고 혈압을 쟀습니다.

    He gave me a chest X-ray and took my blood pressure.

59) 그는 제게 네 시간마다 이 알약을 먹으라고 말했습니다.

    He told me to take these pills every four hours.

60) 당신은 그 환자가 치료될 수 있다고 생각하십니까?
Do you think the patient can be cured?

61) 그들은 지난밤에 그를 수술 했습니다.
They operated on him last night.

62) 그는 수혈이 필요했습니다.
He needed a blood trans- fusion.

63) 제 삼촌은 작년에 심장마비를 일으켰습니다.
My uncle had a heart attack last year.

64) 그들은 심장 전문가를 불러야 했습니다.
They had to call in a heart specialist.

65) 의사는 뭐라고 했습니까?
What did the doctor say?

66) 의사는 제게 많은 운동을 하라고 충고했습니다.
The doctor advised me to get plenty of exercise.

67) 의사는 제가 창백해 보인다고 말했습니다.
The doctor said I look pale.

68) 제가 건강해지기를 원한다면, 저는 담배 피는 것을 끊어야 합니다.
If I want to be healthy, I have to stop smoking cigarettes.

69) 그 내과 의사는 흡연이 제 건강에 해롭다고 말했습니다.
The physician said smoking is harmful to my health.

70) 이것은 모기에 물린 것일 뿐 입니다. 걱정할 것 없습니다.
It's just a mosquito bite. There's nothing to worry about.

II. Everyday English

10. School

Useful Expressions

1. 재학 및 출신학교

What college do you study at?
Which university did you go to?
I go to Indiana University.
What year are you in?
I'm a senior in college.
What did you major in at college?
What school did you graduate from?
I graduated from high school three years ago.
I majored in law at both undergraduate and graduate levels.
Have you ever studied abroad?
What degree do you hold?

2. 수강신청과 수업

Where can I get a course description booklet?
Which course would you like to take?
How much is it per credit?
May I drop the course during the semester?
What are the minimum credit hours to be taken per semester?
His lectures are very enthusiastic.
Her lectures are interesting, but she never seems to have a point.

3. 시험과 성적

How was your exam?

II. Everyday English

How did you do on your exam?
Exam questions are all objective.
This will be an essay test.
I just marked the answer sheet randomly.
I did terrible on this test.
The questions were a lot easier than I expected.
I got an A in English.
He is a cut above the others.
She's doing very well at school
She got decent grade in English.
Attendance accounts for 10% of your grade.
He flunked English.
I have an M.S. in electronics.

4. 기숙사와 학교생활

Does your school have dormitories?
What is the dorm fee per semester?
Is there a cafeteria for students in the dorm?
Can I stay in the dorm during the vacation, too?
Were you involved in any club activities?
My favorite subject was political science.
I have a lot of good memories from my college days.
He earned his way through college.
I'm short of money because of my school expenses.

Speaking in English

1) 어느 대학에 다니십니까?

   Which college are you attending?

2) UCLA에 다니고 있습니다.

   I'm attending UCLA.

3) 무얼 전공하십니까?

   What are you majoring in?

4) 교육학을 전공하고 있습니다.

   I'm majoring in Education.

5) 몇 학년입니까?

   What grade are you in?

6) 어느 학교를 나오셨습니까?

   What school did you go to?

7) 이번 학기에는 몇 과목이나 수강신청을 했습니까?

   How many courses are you taking this semester?

8) 19학점을 수강하고 있어요.

   I'm taking 19 credits.

9) 영어시험에서 100점을 받았습니다.

   I got a hundred on the English test.

10) 공부를 해야겠어요.

    I better hit the books.

11) 나는 오늘 미팅했어요.

    I had a blind date today.

II. Everyday English

12) 아르바이트하는 학생들이 많아요.
    Many students are working at part time jobs.

13) 저는 국립순천대학교 졸업생입니다.
    I'm a graduate of Sunchon National University.

14) 그는 제 학교 선배입니다.
    He's ahead of me in school.

15) 순천고등학교가 제 모교입니다.
    Suncheon High School is my alma mater.

16) 그녀는 고등학교를 갓 나왔습니다.
    She's just finished high school.

17) 6개월만 있으면 졸업하게 돼요.
    I've got six months to go until graduation.

18) 그는 대학중퇴자입니다.
    He is a college drop out.

19) 학창 시절에 나는 그 사람과 하숙방을 같이 썼어요.
    I shared the boarding room with him in my school days.

20) 그는 대학에서 퇴학당했어요.
    He was kicked out of the university.

21) 그는 고학으로 대학을 나왔어요.
    He worked his way through college.

22) 그녀는 논평에서 1등 상을 탔어요.
    She won the first prize in a debate.

23) 컴퓨터 강좌에 신청하셨어요? (이름만 적어 넣는 신청)
    Did you sign up for a computer class?

II. Everyday English

24) 아르바이트를 하고 있나요?

   Do you have a part time job?

25) 나는 결강하고 싶지 않습니다.

   I don't want to cut class.

26) 그는 수업 준비하느라 바쁩니다.

   He's busy preparing for class.

27) 네 머리로는 아마 답을 못 구할걸?

   You will never get the answer.

28) 아, 그 문제에 대한 답을 알겠어요.

   Oh, I know the answer to that problem.

29) 그는 아직도 지난 학기에 받은 좋지 않은 성적에 집착하고 있어요.

   He's still hung up on the bad grades he got last semester.

30) 그는 그 작품에 만점을 주었습니다.

   He rated the work a "10".

31) 학위를 얻으려고 공부하는 중입니다.

   I'm working for my degree.

32) 저는 수학적인 머리가 없는 것 같아요.

   I don't think I have a mathematical brain.

33) 나는 장학금을 신청했어요.

   I applied for a scholarship.

34) 그는 예일대학에 입학할 만큼 높은 점수를 얻었어요.

   He got scored high enough to attend Yale University.

35) 이건 제게 어려운 학과였어요.

   This has been a hard course for me.

II. Everyday English

36) 우리는 그것을 암기하지 않으면 안 되었어요.

   We had to learn it by heart.

37) 종일 공부를 했더니 넌더리가 나는군요.

   I've been studying all day, and I'm sick and tired of it.

38) 시험이 박두했어요.

   The examinations are almost here!

39) 이제 공부를 좀 해야 할 것 같아요.

   I think I have to hit the books now.

40) 그는 학교 성적이 매우 좋아진 것 같아요.

   He seems to be getting on very well at school.

41) 난 그 실험결과에 큰 기대를 걸고 있어요.

   I have high expectations for the outcome of the experiment.

42) 학교 얘기가 났으니 말인데, 이번 학기의 학점은 어때요?

   Speaking of school, how are your grades this term?

43) 모두가 좋은 성적을 얻었다고 발표하게 되어 기쁘군요.

   I'm pleased to announce that everybody got good results.

44) 그의 강의는 재미있지만 결코 목적이 없는 것 같아요.

   His lectures are interesting but he never seems to come to the point.

45) 그녀는 반에서 1등이에요.

   She is at the top of her class.

46) 그녀는 동급생 중에서도 두드러집니다.

   She is a cut above her classmates.

47) 내가 우리 반에서 제일 뒤떨어진 것 같아요.

   Looks like I'm far behind my classmates.

II. Everyday English

48) 그는 물리학에 뛰어난 사람이에요.

    He's very good at physics.

49) 누구나 시험을 잘 보았어요.

    Everyone has passed the exam with flying colors.

50) 열심히 공부하지 않으면 영어에서 합격점을 따기 어려울걸요.

    If you don't study hard, you won't be able to succeed at English.

51) 만일 수업에 늦으면 어떻게 하지요?

    What if we're late for the class?

52) 그의 바보 같은 질문이 선생님의 신경을 몹시 건드린 거예요.

    His foolish question exas- perated the teacher.

53) 게시판에 뭐라고 씌어 있어요?

    What does the board say?

54) 그녀는 내가 영어를 가르쳐 주는 대가로 나에게 피아노를 가르쳐 줘요.

    She is giving me piano lessons in exchange for her English classes.

55) 나는 맨 뒷자리에 앉기를 좋아해요.

    I like to sit way in the back.

56) 학생회관에서 오늘 저녁 6시에 여학생 파티가 있습니다. (참고: 남학생만의 파티)

    A hen party at six tonight at the students' hall. (cf: stag party)

57) 친구의 영어 테이프를 복사하고 있어요.

    I'm copying my friend's English tapes.

58) 너희들은 항상 붙어 다니는구나.

    You always stick together.

59) 그 선생님은 천하태평이에요.
   He's an easy-going teacher.

60) 내가 들은 과목은 나한테 너무 어려웠어요.
   The course I took was too hard for me.

61) 내가 아는 바로는 그분은 교수예요.
   As far as I know, he is a professor.

62) 또 학교에 가야 되는구나. (방학이 끝날 때 가기 싫다는 뜻)
   It is time to go.

63) 열심히 공부하는 게 나쁠 건 하나도 없어요.
   There's nothing wrong with hard work.

64) 너희들은 왜 방과 후에도 잡혀 있니?
   Why are you being kept in after work?

65) 그는 밤중까지 공부를 해요.
   He is burning the midnight oil.

66) 시험결과는 어떻게 되었나요?
   How did the test turn out?

67) 그녀는 한국사에 정통합니다.
   She has a great knowledge of Korean history.

68) 문학사 학위를 갖고 있습니다.
   I have a Bachelor of Arts degree.

69) 당신은 대학에서 어떤 성적을 받았습니까?
   What kind of grades did you get in college?

70) 존은 과외 활동을 합니다. 그는 축구팀에 있습니다.
   John has extracurricular acti- vities. He's on the football team.

II. Everyday English

11. Restaurant

Useful Expressions

1. 예약

   Could I make a reservation?
   Do you have ten seats together?
   Please reserve a table for four at seven tonight.
   I'd like to make a reservation for five at six o'clock.
   I'd like to have a table with a nice view, please.
   I'm wondering whether we need a reservation for dinner.

2. 주문

   Can I see the menu, please?
   I'd like to know what today's special is.
   What's the chef's specialty?
   Would you make a recommendation?
   Waiter, can you take our order, please?
   T-born steak with salad, please.
   Make it two, please.
   I'll have the same.
   I want to have a drink before my meal.
   Can I take your order now?
   How do you like your beef?
   I'd like it well-done.
   What would you like as an appetizer, sir?
   I'd like a vanilla ice cream, please.

3. 식성과 음식의 맛

I think you're very fussy about what you eat.
I don't like foreign food.
I'm allergic to pork.
I don't like oily food.
I'm a picky eater.
It's sweet, sour, and delicious.
This is too greasy and spicy.
This fruit tasted like lemon.
It tastes as good as it looks.
This cake is yummy!

4. 계 산

May I have the check, please?
Could you charge this to my room?
This is my treat.
It's my turn to pay.
Let it be my turn to treat you.
You may treat me next time.
You're my guest today.
Let's split the bill, shall we?
Let's share the bill.
Let's go fifty-fifty on the bill.
Let's pay separately today.
There's a mistake in the bill.
I wonder if the bill is correct.
Is the tip included?

Speaking in English

1) 좋은 식당을 알고 계십니까?
   Do you know of any good restaurants?

2) 특별히 마음에 드는 식당이라도 있으세요?
   Do you have any particular restaurant in mind?

3) 메인스트리트에 한 곳 있습니다. 그곳의 프랑스 음식 맛이 아주 좋습니다.
   There's one on Main Street. They serve excellent French food.

4) 이 식당에서는 좋은 음식을 제공합니다.
   They serve fine food in this restaurant.

5) 2인용 테이블로 해드릴까요?
   A table for two, sir?

6) 실례합니다. 이곳에 누가 앉으세요?
   Excuse me. Is this seat taken (occupied)?

7) 4인용으로 해주세요. 친구들이 올 겁니다.
   Make that four, please. We're expecting friends.

8) 점심으로 뭘 먹을까요?
   What should we try for lunch?

9) 새우튀김을 먹어본 (맛보신) 적이 있나요?
   Have you ever tried (tasted) fried shrimp?

10) 한국음식을 좋아하세요?
    Do you like Korean food?

11) 가장 좋아하는 한국음식은 뭔가요?
    What's your favorite Korean food?

12) 무슨 종류의 한국 음식을 드시겠어요?

What kind of Korean food would you like to try(have)?

13) 저희들의 특별요리는 숯불갈비입니다.

Our specialty is charcoaled galbi.

14) 전 정말 모르겠어요. 저 대신 주문해 주세요.

I really don't know. Why don't you order for me?

15) 좋아요. 불고기를 드시는 게 어때요? 로스트비프 같은 거예요.

O.K. How about trying bulgogi? It's like roast beef.

16) 좋아요. 당신이 주문하는 대로 할게요.

Fine. Whatever you say.

17) 주문하시겠습니까, 손님?

Are you ready to order now, sir?

18) 무엇을 드시겠습니까?

What would you like to eat?

19) 토마토 수프로 주세요.

I'd like a bowl of tomato soup, please.

20) 웨이터가 우리 주문을 받으려고 서두르는 것 같습니다.

The waiter seems to be in a hurry to take our order.

21) 스테이크와 생선 중 어느 것을 드시겠습니까?

Which would you rather have? Steak or fish?

22) 저는 제 스테이크를 잘 익혀 주기 바랍니다.

I want my steak well-done.

23) 어떤 종류의 야채를 드시겠습니까?

What kinds of vegetables do you have?

II. Everyday English

24) 저는 으깬 감자와 강낭콩을 먹겠습니다.
    I'll have mashed potatoes and green beans.

25) 네. 토마토 수프, 로스트 비프, 그리고 메쉬 포테이토를 주세요.
    Yes. I'll have tomato soup, roast beef and mashed potatoes.

26) 무얼 먹었으면 좋겠어요?
    What do you recommend?

27) 오늘 특별요리가 뭐죠?
    What's the special of the day?

28) 스테이크는 어떻게 해드릴까요.
    How do you want the steak?

29) 바짝 구워(덜 익혀, 중간쯤 익혀) 주세요.
    Well-done (Rare, Medium), please.

30) 마실 것은 어떻게 하시겠어요?
    Anything to drink?

31) 커피 한잔 드시겠습니까?
    Would you care for a cup of coffee?

32) 커피에 설탕이나 크림을 넣으세요?
    Do you take sugar or cream in your coffee?

33) 저는 설탕을 조금만 넣어서 블랙으로 하죠.
    I like mine black with pinch of sugar.

34) 물이면 되겠어요.
    A glass of water will be fine.

35) 그리고 손님은요?
    And you, sir?

II. Everyday English

36) 나도 같은 것으로 하겠습니다.
   Same here.

37) 저 여자 분이 하시는 걸로 하겠습니다.
   I'll have what she's having.

38) 당신은 세 가지 맛을 선택할 수 있습니다.
   You have a choice of three flavors of ice cream.

39) 우리는 바닐라, 초콜릿, 딸기가 있습니다.
   We have vanilla, chocolate, and strawberry.

40) 얼마나 자주 외식을 하십니까?
   How often do you eat out?

41) 점심은 내가 사죠.
   Lunch is on me.

42) 각자 부담합시다.
   Let's split the bill.

43) 마실 것은 내가 내죠.
   Drinks are on me.

44) 그게 전부인가요?
   Is that all?

45) 여기서 드실 건가요, 아니면 가지고 가실건가요?
   For here or to go?

46) 프랜치 프라이 큰 것, 가지고 갈 겁니다.
   Two large french fries to go.

47) 아가씨, 계산서 좀 가져 오세요.
   Miss, may I have the check?

II. Everyday English

48) 당신 때문에 줄이 이동이 안됩니다.
    You're holding up the line.

49) 이 우유(고기)가 상했어요.
    This milk (meat) has gone bad.

50) 이 빵이 오래되어 딱딱해요.
    This bread's stale.

51) 이 맥주가 김이 빠졌군요.
    This beer is flat.

52) 달걀이 상했군요.
    These eggs are rotten.

53) 이 크림이 상했군요.
    This cream is sour

54) 소금 좀 건네주시겠습니까?
    Would you please pass the salt?

55) 당신은 지금 후식 드실 준비가 되셨습니까?
    Are you ready for your dessert now?

56) 이 나이프는 더럽습니다. 깨끗한 것으로 가져다 주시겠습니까?
    This knife is dirty. Would you bring me a clean one, please?

57) 간밤의 저녁 식사가 어땠어요?
    How did you enjoy your dinner last night?

58) 아주 좋았어요.
    It was very good.

59) 형편없었습니다.
    It was terrible.

60) 음식도 차고 서비스는 엉망이고 값은 터무니없었거든요.
The food was cold, the service was bad and the meals were overpriced.

12. Shopping

Useful Expressions

1. 물건 구입

I want something made of leather.
Could you help me find one like this?
Please show me some wool sweaters.
I'm looking for a gift for my daughter.
I like that one. Can I see it?
Let me see the one on display.

2. 치수

It's too tight in the shoulder.
These shoes fit me perfectly.
It seems to be too big for me.
Do you have this shirt in a smaller size?
Could you show me one size up (down)?

3. 재질과 유형

What kind of material is it?
Is this waterproof?
What's it made of?
Is this bag durable?
Which color looks better on me?
Long skirts are in vogue now.

4. 가격

How much is it?
How much does it cost?
What's the regular price?
What's the price after the discount?
How much will it be with tax?
Is the price as marked? Is it reasonable?
Don't you have anything cheaper?
Would you give me a discount?
Can you give a discount if I buy five?
Will you reduce the price if I buy them in cash?

5. 계산

How much will it cost?
It's twenty dollars plus tax.
Will you add these up for me?
Cash or check?
I will pay by credit card.
Does the price include the service charge?
Put it on my account, please.
Let me have a receipt, please.

6. 반품 또는 환불

Can I return this if it doesn't fit?
I'd like to return this because it's broken.
Would you exchange it for another?
Could I have a refund on this?

II. Everyday English

Speaking in English

1) 도와 드릴까요?

   May I help you?

2) 누가 도와드리고 있나요?

   Are you being helped?

3) 이미 안내를 받고 있어요.

   I'm being helped.

4) 한국적인 것을 사고 싶습니다.

   I want to buy something Korean.

5) 아뇨. 그냥 구경만 하는 겁니다.

   No, I'm just browsing.

6) 아니 괜찮아요. 그냥 구경하고 있어요.

   No, thank you. I'm just looking.

7) 도움이 필요하시면 부르세요. 제 이름은 켄입니다.

   If you need any help, my name is Ken.

8) 네. 검정 가죽 잠바를 찾고 있는데요.

   Yes, I am looking for a black leather jacket.

9) 저 외투가 맘에 드는데요. 얼마입니까?

   I'm interested in that top coat. How much is it?

10) 싸이즈가 얼마입니까?

    What size do you wear?

11) 대 짜리(큰 것)요.

    I need a large.

12) 좀 입어봤으면 좋겠는데요.

   I'd like to try some on.

13) (옷) 갈아입는 곳이 어디죠?

   Where's the dressing room?

14) 이건 어떻습니까?

   How do you like this one?

15) 색깔이나 모양이 맘에 들지 않습니다.

   I don't like the color or the pattern.

16) 얼마입니까?

   How much do I owe you?

17) 이 넥타이들은 얼마입니까?

   How much are these ties?

18) 5불 50센트 짜리부터 있습니다.

   Those are five fifty and up.

19) $ 5.50에 세금을 더하면 됩니다.

   You owe me $ 5.50 plus tax.

20) 또 더 필요한 건 없으세요?

   Will there be anything else?

21) 저 셔츠 좀 봅시다.

   Let me see that shirt.

22) 여기 있습니다.

   Here you are.

23) 이것도 사겠습니다.

   I'll take this, too.

II. Everyday English

24) 배달해 줍니까?

    Do you deliver?

25) 네 배달해 드립니다. 어디로 배달해 드릴까요?

    Yes, we do. Where do you want it delivered?

26) 현금인가요, 카드인가요?

    Will this be cash or charge?

27) 카드로요.

    Charge.

28) 마스터 카드를 받나요?

    Do you accept Master card?

29) 죄송합니다만 마스터 카드는 받지 않고 비자만 받습니다.

    I'm sorry, we don't take Master card, only Visa.

30) 몇 시까지 여세요?

    How late are you open?

31) 토요일은 상점시간이 어떻게 됩니까?

    What are your hours on Saturday?

32) 평일에는 6시까지이고 주말 에는 5시까지 엽니다.

    We're open till six on weekdays and till five on weekends.

33) 하루 24시간 엽니다.

    We're open twenty four hours a day.

34) 내일 문을 여십니까?

    Will you be open tomorrow?

35) 내일은 국경일이기 때문에 온 종일 문을 닫습니다.

    No, it's national holiday. We'll be closed all day.

II. Everyday English

36) 책임자가 누구입니까?

    Who's in charge of customer complaints?

37) 돈으로 반환해 주셨으면 하는 데요.

    I'd like a refund.

38) 영수증을 가지고 계세요?

    Do you have a receipt?

39) 돈을 돌려주세요.

    I want my money back.

40) 다른 것과 교환할 수 있을까요?

    Can I exchange it for another one?

41) 어제 이 토스터를 어제 이곳에서 샀는데 고장이네요.

    I bought this toaster here yesterday, but it doesn't work.

42) 좋습니다. 어떻게 해 보도록 하죠.

    All right. I'll see what I can do.

43) 그거 얼마주고 샀어요?

    How much did you pay for it?

44) 똑같은 것을 나는 85불 줬거든요.

    I paid $85.00 for the same thing.

45) 그건 바가지예요.

    That's a rip-off.

46) 정말 내가 바가지를 쓴 것 같네요.

    I guess I really got ripped- off.

47) 무슨 근거로 그렇게 얘기하죠?

    What makes you say so?

II. Everyday English

48) 내 생각에는 그 친구가 나에게 제 값보다 훨씬 더 받은 것 같아요.
    I think he charged me more than it's worth.

49) 그 사람은 나에게 돈을 너무 많이 받았어요.
    He charged me too much.

50) 제값보다 더 많이 매겨져 있어.
    It's overpriced.

51) 이 블라우스와 이 신을 교환하고 싶습니다.
    I'd like to exchange this blouse and these shoes.

52) 한 번에 하나씩 처리하도록 하지요. 가격표(영수증)를 좀 보여주실까요?
    I can only handle one item at a time. May I see the sales slips?

53) 미안합니다만 제게 없는데요.
    I'm sorry, I don't have them.

54) 가격 장부를 대조해 봐야겠습니다.
    I'll have to check the price book.

55) 오래 걸립니까?
    Will that take long?

56) 아니요. 잠깐이면 됩니다.
    No. It just takes a minute.

57) 저는 옷을 좀 살 필요가 있어서 쇼핑을 갑니다.
    I'm going shopping because I need to buy some clothes.

58) 이 셔츠가 맞지 않는다면, 나중에 다시 가져와도 됩니까?
    If this shirt doesn't fit, may I bring it back later?

59) 당신은 어느 사이즈의 구두를 신습니까?
    What size shoes do you wear?

II. Everyday English

60) 그 옷은 당신에게 잘 어울립니다.

    That suit looks very good on you.

61) 이 드레스는 비단으로 만들어졌죠, 그렇지 않습니까?

    This dress is made of silk, isn't it?

62) 저는 이 스웨터를 입어보고 싶습니다.

    I'd like to try on this sweater.

63) 저는 새 차 사는데 관심이 있습니다.

    I'm interested in buying a new car.

64) 저 전기다리미의 가격이 얼마입니까?

    What's the price of that electric iron?

65) 이 바닥 깔개는 얼마입니까?

    How much is this rug?

66) 이 치약은 오늘 세일을 합니까?

    Is this toothpaste on sale today?

67) 저것은 아름다운 가죽지갑 입니다만, 너무 비쌉니다.

    That's a beautiful leather wallet, but it costs too much.

68) 제가 얼마를 지불해야 됩니까?

    How much do I owe you?

69) 20달러 지폐를 드린다면 거스름돈이 있습니까?

    Do you have change for a twenty-dollar bill?

70) 그 점원은 제가 원하는 것을 찾도록 도와주었습니다.

    The clerk helped me find what I wanted.

13. Directions

Useful Expressions

1. 길 묻기

Could you show me the way?
Would you tell me how to get there?
I got lost. Are you familiar with this area?
Which street am I on now?
How many blocks is it to the Sejong Center?
Where can I find the bank?

2. 길 안내하기

Are you from around here?
Keep going along this street.
Go west for two blocks.
Go straight, and turn right at the signal.
I'm going in the same direction. I'll go with you.
You'll find the building on your right.

3. 거리와 소요시간

How far is it?
How much farther do I have to walk?
How long do you think it'll take?
It's about a five-minute walk.
It's about a ten-minute ride.

4. 대중교통

Where does bus No. 33 go?
Can I take this bus to Seoul Station?
What bus number should I catch to City Hall?
How often does this bus run?
No. 50 bus runs every ten minutes.
Can I get there by subway?
Which line goes to Central Park?
Where can I buy the ticket?
Where do I have to transfer?
Please transfer at the third stop.
I'd like to reserve a seat on the 10:00 train to Seoul, please.

5. 자동차

Fill her up with regular, please.
I'd like to wipe the windshield.
My car's making strange noises.
My car is fuel efficient.
I had a flat tire this morning.

6. 교통 상황

I was late due to bumper to bumper traffic.
I was caught in an awful traffic jam.
Many cars cutting in cause heavy traffic.
There's a car accident farther up the road, and it's tying up traffic.

II. Everyday English

Speaking in English

1) 어느 쪽으로 가십니까?
   Where are you going?

2) 어느 쪽이 남쪽이죠?
   Which way is south?

3) 어린이 대공원까지 몇 정거장을 가야 합니까?
   How many stops away is the Children's Grand Park?

4) 실례합니다, 선생님. 제게 정보를 좀 주실 수 있습니까?
   Excuse me, sir. Can you give me some information?

5) 피치 스트리트가 어디에 있는 가요?
   Can you tell me where Peach Street is?

6) 앞으로 곧장 두 블록만 가면 됩니다.
   It's two blocks straight ahead.

7) 극장은 어느 방향입니까?
   Which direction is it to the theater?

8) 다음 모퉁이에서 오른쪽으로 도세요.
   Turn right at the next corner.

9) 대학까지는 얼마나 멉니까?
   How far is it to the university?

10) 여기에서는 먼 거리입니다.
    It's a long way from here.

11) 그 학교는 모퉁이 돌아서 바로 있습니다.
    The school is just around the corner.

II. Everyday English

12) 그 식당은 호텔에서 길 건너편에 있습니다.
    The restaurant is across the street from the hotel.

13) 당신은 쉽게 찾을 수 있을 것입니다.
    You can't miss it.

14) 혹시 쿠퍼 씨 전화번호를 알고 계십니까?
    Do you happen to know Mr. Cooper's telephone number?

15) 가장 가까운 공중전화가 어디 있는지 말씀해 주실 수 있습니까?
    Could you tell me where the nearest public telephone is?

16) 이 길로 가야 합니까? 아니면 저 길로 가야 합니까?
    Should I go this way, or that way?

17) 저 길로 두 블록 가서, 왼쪽으로 도세요.
    Go that way for two blocks, then turn left.

18) 그 곳으로 가는 약도를 좀 그려 주시겠습니까?
    Could you draw a map to get there for me?

19) 길 건너편에 있습니다.
    It's across the street.

20) 길을 안내할게요. 저도 같은 방향이니까요.
    I'll show you the way. I'm going in the same direction.

21) 사람 참 많군요!
    What a crowd of people!

22) 사람들이 꽤 많네요!
    Quite a crowd, isn't it?

23) 수원을 가려면 어떻게 가죠?
    How can I get to Suwon?

II. Everyday English

24) 서울에서 남쪽으로 약 20마 일 떨어져 있습니다.

    It's about 20 miles south of Seoul.

25) 지하철을 타세요.

    Take a subway train, please.

26) 그 열차는 급행입니까, 완행입니까?

    Is the train an express or a local?

27) 어디서 열차를 바꿔 타야 합니까?

    Where should I transfer trains?

28) 서울역에서 차를 바꿔 타세요.

    Transfer at Seoul Station.

29) 우리들이 순천역을 지나가면 지나간다고 알려 주세요.

    Would you point out the Suncheon Station as we go by?

30) 버스 정류소가 어디에 있습니까?

    Where is the bus stop?

31) 서울행 버스가 맞습니까?

    Is this the right bus to Seoul?

32) 어느 버스가 중심가로 갑니까?

    Which bus goes to the town center?

33) 지금부터 몇 번째 정류장입니 까?

    How many stops from here is it?

34) 내릴 때가 되면 알려 주시겠어요?

    Will you tell me when to get off?

35) 버스가 저쪽으로 건너가서 정차합니다.

    The bus will stop over there.

II. Everyday English

36) 택시를 잡아탑시다.

    Let's catch a cab.

37) 택시 타는 데가 어디입니까?

    Where's the taxi stand?

38) 택시 요금은 얼마죠?

    How much is the taxi fare?

39) 때로는 택시기사들이 일부러 멀리 돌아가기도 하죠.

    Sometimes, taxi drivers take the long way on purpose.

40) 시간이 얼마나 걸린다고 생각하세요?

    How long do you think it'll take?

41) 길을 잃었습니다. 여기가 어디죠?

    I'm lost. Where am I?

42) 방향을 모르겠습니다.

    I have no sense of direction.

43) 방향감각을 잃었습니다.

    I lost my sense of direction.

44) 위치가 어디쯤 됩니까?

    What's the location?

45) 어느 길을 따라가야 하는지 이 지도를 보고 좀 가르쳐 주세요.

    Please show me on this map which street I should follow.

46) 어느 길이 종로로 가는 지름 길인가요?

    Which way is the shortcut to Jongro?

47) 어머! 너를 이런 데서 만나다니!

    Fancy meeting you here!

II. Everyday English

48) 위급한 경우에는 112번을 돌리세요.
    In case of emergency, dial 112.

49) 이 근처에 공중전화가 있습니까?
    Is there a pay phone around here?

50) 이 근처의 다른 호텔을 하나 추천해 주시겠습니까?
    Could you recommend another hotel near here?

14. Traveling

Useful Expressions

1. 비자 신청

Could you tell me what your purpose is in applying for a visa?
I've wanted to be a professor ever since I was little. I want to come back to my country and have a chance to apply what I learn.
Who is going to support you during your stay in the United States?
My father will finance all my expenses.

2. 항공편 예약

I'd like to make a reservation to Seattle for July 5th.
Please let me know the departure times of the flights to Seattle tomorrow.
Is it a direct fly to New York?
I'll take that flight, and could you book me on that flight?
Is that one way or round trip?
Do you want first class or economy?
It flies to Los Angeles via Anchorage.
I'd like to confirm my reservation on Flight 008.

3. 탑승 수속

Would you tell me where the KAL counter is?
Please be present at gate 5 twenty minutes before departure time.
I'd like to check in this suitcase.
May I carry this bag on board?
I'd like a window seat in the non-smoking section, please.

II. Everyday English

Is the plane due on schedule?
It'll be delayed about an hour due to the fog.

4. 비행기 내

I'd like to sit together with my companion.
Would you mind changing your seat with me?
This flight is now leaving for Vancouver via Narita.
We are taking off shortly. Please fasten your seat belt.
The emergency exits are located on either side of the plane next to the wings.
Can I have something to drink?
Would you show me the duty-free catalogue, please?
What time will we be landing?
I have to catch a connecting flight to Houston.
My flight on your line was delayed and I missed a connecting flight.
You have to arrange accommodation for me.

5. 도착지 공항

What is the purpose of your visit?
I'm here to go sightseeing.
Where can I pick up my luggage from KAL flight 201?
Carousel 5.
My bag didn't come out on the conveyer belt.

6. 호텔

Do you have any vacancies tonight?
I'd like a room with an ocean view.
I'd like to make a reservation for three nights for two.
How much does it cost per day?

Is breakfast included in this rate?
I'd like to check a room reserved under the name of Patrick.
Can I have some extra towels?
Would you recommend a nice French restaurant?

7. 관광지에서

What are the major tourist attractions in this city?
What's the admission fee to the museum?
I'd like a tour brochure, please.
The scenery is beautiful beyond expression.
May I take a picture with your children?
Would you take my picture, please?

II. Everyday English

Speaking in English

1) 탑승권을 좀 보여 주시겠습니까?
   May I see your boarding pass, please?

2) 이 가방을 어떻게 할까요?
   What should I do with this bag?

3) 의자 밑이나 머리 위에 있는 통 속에 놓아두십시오.
   Please put it under your seat or in the overhead bin.

4) 몇 시간 더 가면 뉴욕에 착륙 합니까?
   How many more hours until we land in New York?

5) 얼마나 더 가야 되죠?
   How much farther is it?

6) 몇 시에 시카고에 착륙할까요?
   What time do we land in Chicago?

7) 비행 중에 저녁식사가 나옵니까?
   Are you going to serve dinner on this flight?

8) 방문 목적은 무엇입니까?
   What's the purpose of your visit?

9) 서울에서 당신의 목적지는 어디입니까?
   What is your destination in Seoul?

10) 고국에 언제 돌아가실 계획입니까?
    When do you plan to return to your home country?

11) 이 나라에 얼마동안 머물 예정이십니까?
    How long are you going to stay in this country?

12) 본부호텔 인 라마다호텔까지 부탁합니다.
   Take me to the Ramada Hotel, the Headquarters. Hotel.

13) 여기서 거리가 얼마나 되지요?
   How far is it from here?

14) 밤 이맘때면 아마 30분쯤 걸릴 겁니다.
   It'll take maybe thirty mi- nutes this time of night.

15) 요금은 얼마나 될까요?
   How much will the fare be?

16) 비행기를 타야 하는데요. 급히 갈 수 없을까요?
   I have to catch a plane. Can't you hurry?

17) 최선을 다해서 가고 있습니다.
   I'm going as fast as I can.

18) 방하나 있습니까?
   I'd like a room, please.

19) 1인용입니까, 2인용입니까?
   Single or double, sir?

20) 언제 들어오시죠?
   When are you checking in?

21) 며칠 밤을 주무실 겁니까, 손님?
   For how many nights, sir?

22) 3일 밤을 지내고 토요일 오전에 나가려고요.
   I'd like to stay 3 nights and check out Saturday morning.

23) 짐꾼이 가방을 운반해 드릴 겁니다.
   The porter will take your bags.

II. Everyday English

24) 방을 나가야 하는 시간이 언제입니까?
    What is the check-out time?

25) 내일 아침 8시에 나가게 될 겁니다.
    I'll be checking out tomorrow morning at eight.

26) 내 방이 엘리베이터에 너무 가까이 있는데 바꿀 수 있을까요?
    My room is too close to the elevator. Can I change it?

27) 죄송합니다. 방이 만원입니다.
    Sorry, sir. We're full.

28) 6시에 내방으로 전화를 해서 좀 깨워주시겠어요?
    Can you give me a wake-up call at six?

29) 관광할 만한 데를 몇 군데 소개해 주시겠습니까?
    Could you suggest some interesting places to visit?

30) 20불 짜리 뿐인데 잔돈으로 거슬러 주시겠어요?
    Can you break a twenty dollar bill?

31) 물론이죠. 1불짜리 여러 개로 드려도 괜찮으시다면.
    Sure, if you don't mind getting a lot of singles.

32) 제가 거슬러 드릴 수 있습니다.
    I can break it for you.

33) 미리 지불하셔야 합니다.
    You have to pay in advance.

34) 전화를 해서 표를 미리 예약 해야겠습니다.
    I'd better call and reserve the tickets in advance.

35) 가셔서 영주하실 계획인가요?
    Are you going to stay there permanently?

II. Everyday English

36) 비행기로 가시나요?

    Are you flying?

37) 어디 가십니까?

    Where are you headed?

38) 뉴욕에 가는 중입니다.

    I'm on my way to New York.

39) 4 주간 휴가입니다.

    I have four weeks off for vacation.

40) 목적지가 어디신가요?

    What's your destination?

41) 금남로로 가려면 어느 쪽으로 가야 합니까?

    Which way do I go to get to Geumnam-ro?.

42) 지금 여기가 금남로입니다.

    You are on Geumnam-ro.

43) 여기서 박물관까지는 얼마나 멉니까?

    How far is the Museum from here?

44) 여기서 약 2블록 정도입니다.

    It's about two blocks from here.

45) 얼마나 자주 뉴욕 행 비행기가 있습니까?

    How often do you have flights to New York?

46) 충분한 돈이 있다면, 저는 해외여행을 하려고 합니다.

    If I have enough money, I'm going to take a trip abroad.

47) 어떻게 가시려고 합니까? 배로 가실 것입니까?

    How are you going? Are you going by boat?

II. Everyday English

48) 배로 가는 것보다 비행기로 가는 것이 더 빠릅니다.
    It's faster to go by plane than by boat.

49) 그 곳에 도착하는 가장 빠른 방법은 무엇입니까?
    What's the quickest way to get there?

50) 6시간 걸리는 비행이었습니다.
    It was a six-hour flight.

51) 태평양 근처는 경치가 아름답습니다.
    The scenery is beautiful near the Pacific Ocean.

52) 기후는 어떻습니까? 온화합니까?
    What kind of climate do you have? Is it mild?

53) 실례합니다. 이 자리에 손님이 있습니까?
    I beg your pardon. Is this seat taken?

54) 길 좀 비켜 주세요!
    Make way for me, please.

55) 서울에서의 속도제한은 얼마 입니까?
    What's the speed limit in Seoul?

56) 운전면허증 있으세요?
    Do you have a driver's license?

57) 이 근처에 주유소가 있습니까?
    Are there any gas stations around here?

58) 이 도시 여행자를 위한 지도를 구하고 싶은데요.
    I want to buy a tourist map of this city.

59) (연료를) 무연으로 한 탱크 가득 채워주세요.
    Fill her(it) up. Unleaded, please.

II. Everyday English

60) 버스는 매시간 정시에 출발 합니다.

A bus departs every hour on the hour.

II. Everyday English

15. Sports

Useful Expressions

1. 일반 운동

    Do you play any sports?
    What are your favorite sports?
    What sports are you into?
    I enjoy playing tennis.
    Exercise is a good way to stay in shape.
    She is good at horse riding.
    I'm interested in mountain climbing.
    I like basketball best of all sports.
    He's not very good at sports.

2. 승패와 성적

    Which team do you think will win?
    Which team are you cheering for?
    Who holds the world record?
    Who was the winner? What's the score?
    We won by a score of 3 to 2.
    We beat the team by 1:0.
    It was a close game.
    The game ended in a tie.
    The defending champions lost the game.
    The Olympic Games are held every four years.

3. 구기 운동

I like to play golf, but I'm not very good at it.
What's your handi(cap)?
What inning is it?
He's batting number 4 in the lineup.
The bases are loaded (full).
What is the player's batting average?
Are you good at tennis?
Should we play singles or doubles?
It's your turn to serve.
Love means zero in tennis.

4. 수영

What style of swimming do you like best?
I like the crawl stroke best.
What style do you usually use?
Can you do the backstroke?
You have to warm up before you go swimming.
I am what we call a hammer.
I can swim like a fish.

5. 스키

I go skiing every winter.
I've just learned to do stem turns.
You cannot be too careful skiing at night.
I'm crazy about skiing, because it gives me great pleasure to glide swiftly down the slopes.

Speaking in English

1) 두 팀이 마지막 회까지 막상 막하였어요.

   The two teams were neck and neck until the last inning.

2) 기아 타이거스가 압도적인 차로 이길 것으로 알았는데요.

   I thought the Kia Tigers would win by a landslide.

3) 저도 그렇게 생각했습니다. 그런데 막판에 가서 정말 호가 지세였죠.

   So did I, but it was really close at the end.

4) 그 말이 가까스로 그 경주에서 우승했어요.

   The horse barely managed to win that race!

5) 알아요. 무승부나 다름없었지요.

   I know! It was almost a dead heat.

6) 우리 팔씨름하자.

   Let's play arm wrestling.

7) 나는 물구나무를 설 수 있다.

   I can stand on my hands.

8) 그 축구경기 보셨어요?

   Did you watch the soccer game?

9) 7:6으로 우리가 이겼어요.

   The score was seven to six in our favor.

10) 한국과 브라질의 축구 경기는 비겼습니다.

    The soccer game between Korea and Brazil was a draw.

11) 3:0으로 기아 타이거스가 이기고 있습니다.

    The score is 3 to nothing in favor of the Kia Tigers.

II. Everyday English

12) 오늘 오후에 중요한 야구경기가 있다던데요. 그곳으로 저를 안내하면 어때요?

    I've heard there is a big baseball game this after- noon. Why don't you take me there?

13) 그 시합 볼 만하던가요?

    Was the game worth watching?

14) 오늘밤 그 경기가 텔레비전에 방영됩니까?

    Is the game on TV tonight?

15) 언제 방송됩니까?

    When is it on?

16) 두고 봐야죠.

    We'll have to wait and see.

17) 경기는 8시에 시작될 겁니다.

    The game is going to start at 8 o'clock.

18) 이 게임은 생방송입니까?

    Is this game live?

19) 당신은 어느 팀을 응원하고 있지요?

    Which team are you rooting for?

20) 그저 약한 쪽을 응원하고 싶어요.

    I just like to root for the underdog.

21) 당신은 얼마나 자주 운동을 하세요?

    How often do you work out?

22) 시합 결과는 어떻게 되었나요?

    How did the game turn out?

II. Everyday English

23) 우리가 3:0으로 승리했어요.
    We won the game 3 to nothing.

24) 우리는 2:5로 패배했어요.
    We lost the game 2 to 5.

25) 스코어는 6:6으로 비겼어요.
    The score was tied, six to six.

26) 경기는 무승부로 끝났습니다.
    The game ended in a tie.

27) 경기는 무승부였어요.
    The game was tied.

28) 야구할 때, 당신의 포지션이 뭡니까?
    When you play baseball, what position do you play?

29) 1루수입니다.
    I play first base.

30) 그는 홈런 8개를 날렸어요.
    He hit eight home runs.

31) 2번 타자는 백 스크린에 맞는 파울볼을 쳤어요.
    The second batter fouled the ball against the screen.

32) (투수인) 난 날카롭게 떨어지는 커브 공을 던져요.
    I pitch sharp breaking curve- balls.

33) 그는 타율이 어떻게 됩니까?
    What is his batting average?

34) 저는 평범한 선수입니다. (보통입니다.)
    I'm an average player.

II. Everyday English

35) 찰리는 올림픽에 나가 보려 합니다.
    Charlie is trying out for the Olympics.

36) 한미 야구전에 많은 사람들이 몰려들었어요.
    A ROK-US baseball tourna- ment drew a large crowd.

37) 야구가 제가 가장 좋아하는 스포츠입니다. 당신은?
    Baseball is my favorite sport. What's your favorite sport?

38) 제 조카는 야구 선수입니다. 그는 포수입니다.
    My nephew is a baseball player. He is a catcher.

39) 그 남자는 야구광이고, 그 여자는 영화광이에요.
    He is a baseball buff while she is a film buff.

40) 그는 운동 기능이 좋다.
    He's got good motor skills.

41) 누구를 가장 좋아하죠?
    Who's your favorite?

42) 하는 것이 타이틀을 뺏길 것 같군.
    Chances are he's going to lose his title.

43) 난 전남드래곤즈의 열렬한 팬이에요. 파이팅, 드래곤즈!
    I'm a keen fan of the Jeonnam Dragons. Go, Dragons!

44) 지금이 찬스(기회)나. 슛해!
    Now is the time. Take a shot!

45) 나는 축구팀의 후보선수예요.
    I'm just a bench warmer on the football team.

46) 승리는 우리의 것입니다.
    The victory is ours.

II. Everyday English

47) 축구경기에는 잠시도 한눈팔 순간이 없어요.
    There's never a dull moment in a soccer game.

48) 제가 주심이었다면 그때 벌칙을 주지는 않았을 거예요.
    If I'd been the referee, I wouldn't have given a penalty then.

49) 당신이 축구했을 때, 어떤 포지션을 맡았습니까?
    When you played football, what position did you play?

50) 우리는 지난밤에 시합을 했습니다. 점수는 6대6으로 비겼습니다.
    We played a game last night. The score was tied six-to-six.

51) 저는 지난밤에 권투 경기에 갔습니다. 좋은 싸움이었어요.
    I went to a boxing match last night. It was a good fight.

52) 제가 육상 팀에 있었을 때, 저는 1/4 마일을 뛰곤 했습니다.
    When I was on the track team, I used to run the quarter mile.

53) 저는 낚시와 사냥을 좋아합니다만, 수영은 좋아하지 않습니다.
    I like fishing and hunting, but I don't like swimming.

54) 제가 가장 좋아하는 겨울 운동은 스키입니다. 저는 스키 클럽에 속해 있습니다.
    My favorite winter sport is skiing. I belong to a ski club.

55) 작년엔 어디로 스키 타러 갔나요?
    Where did you go skiing last year?

56) 오늘 오후에 경마에 가는 것에 관심 있으십니까?
    Would you be interested in going to the horse races this afternoon?

57) 배우기 가장 힘든 것은 훌륭한 패자가 되는 것입니다.
    The hardest thing to learn is to be a good loser.

58) 공평하게 하세요. 게임의 규칙에 따라 경기하세요.
    Be fair. Play according to the rules of the game.

II. Everyday English

59) 우리 가족은 지난 여름에 야영을 갔습니다. 우리는 새 텐트를 사야만 했습니다.
    Our family went camping last summer. We had to buy a new tent.

60) 오늘 오후에 우리는 운동하러 체육관에 갔습니다. 우리는 역도를 했습니다.
    This afternoon we went to the gym for a workout. We lifted weights.

61) 제 근육이 역도를 해서 쑤십니다.
    My muscles are sore from lifting weights.

62) 골프에 대한 거라면 그 사람 못 당할 걸요.
    When it comes to golf, you can't beat him.

63) 그는 요즘에 골프에 빠졌어요.
    He takes to golf these days.

64) 얼마나 멀리 수영할 수 있나요?
    How far can you swim?

65) 이 강을 수영해서 건너갈 수 있습니다.
    I can swim across this river.

66) 나는 형편없어요.
    I'm terrible.

67) 테니스 클럽에 가입이 되어 있나요?
    Do you belong to a tennis club?

68) 자네 점수를 기입했나? (당구칠 때 등)
    Did you mark your score?

69) 그 사람 참 잘 달리는군요.
    He is jet-propelled.

70) 그는 발이 빨라요.
    He runs like a deer.

III. Sports Activities

1. Sporting Spirit
2. Baseball
3. Swimming
4. Basketball
5. Volleyball
6. Soccer
7. American Football
8. Camping
9. Tennis
10. Mountaineering
11. Skiing
12. Skating
13. Golf
14. The Olympics

1. Sporting Spirit

Actual Scene

A: 너의 축구팀이 준결승전 경기를 한다고 들었어. 언제니?
   I heard that your soccer team will play in a semi-final match. When is it?

B: 4월 5일 오후 2시에 열릴거야.
   It'll be held on April 5th at 2 p.m.

A: 얼굴표정이 왜 그래? 그것에 대해 재미나지(흥분되지) 않니?
   Why the long face? Aren't you excited about it?

B: 나도 재미나. 그러나 Badgers 팀에 어떻게 전략을 세워야할지 모르겠어.
   I am, but I have no idea how to plan a strategy against the Badgers.

A: 뭐가 문제야?
   What's the problem?

B: 우리 팀에 비해 그들은 공격이 더 강해.
   Compared to our team, they have a stronger offense.

A: 걱정 마. 너의 팀은 수비가 우수하잖아. 나는 너희 팀이 이길 거라고 믿어.
   Don't worry. Your team has an excellent defense. I'm sure you can win the game.

A: 일본과 아랍에미리트가 얼마 전 1대 1로 비겼어.
   Japan tied United Arab Emirates 1-1 the other day.

B: 정말? 그게 한국 축구팀에 무슨 의미지?
   Really? What does that mean for the Korean soccer team?

III. Sports Activities

A: 한국이 결승진출이 확실해졌어.

It made sure Korea makes it to the finals.

B: 그거 듣기 좋군.

That sounds good.

A: 한국 파이팅!

Korea fighting!

B: 오, 그 말을 영어로 할 때는 "Go Korea!"라고 해야 돼.

Oh, when you say it in English, you should say "Go Korea!"

III. Sports Activities

Learning Terms

World Cup / World Baseball Classic
winner / loser
offense / defense
sportsmanship
hard knocks
forget oneself

"When you're as great as I am, it's hard to be humble."
- Muhammad Ali

Sport and Sporting Spirit

England is the home of sports. Many of the games now played all over the world started in Britain. We have a proverb, "All work and no play makes Jack a dull boy." We do not think that play is more important than work; we think that Jack will do his work better if he plays as well, so he is encouraged to do both. Most people would feel that life was hardly worth living if they could not enjoy their favorite sport in the evenings, or on the weekends. Certainly, in ordinary times, the average man is more interested in games and sports than in politics. The average university students may not be able to tell you the name of the Foreign Minister, but he is able to tell you which team won the football or basketball championship last year.

What is a sportsman? He is the one who is interested in sport. But that is only one meaning of the word. Even if a person is not interested in any sport, and has no time to play games, he may have the 'sporting spirit'. This 'sporting spirit' is something that develops in people as they play games, though a person may have it who plays no game. It is the ability to endure hard knocks without getting angry, the ability to smile in times of danger and hardship, the ability to win without boasting afterwards, and to lose without complaining. A sportsman forgets himself in his loyalty to his team. He does not lose heart when the game is going against him, he goes on fighting when the battle seems already lost.

Some people hate playing if there is no crowd to applaud them, some play only to win prizes, and others are unwilling to play against stronger opponents for fear of defeat. Such people are not sportsmen in the best sense of the word, but if they go on playing they may become sportsmen in time. We should all try to become 'good losers', to accept our disappointments cheerfully. Everyone had disappointments at some time; sportsmen smile when they[1] occur and are never disheartened by them.

---

1) disappointments

2. Baseball

Actual Scene

A: 여보세요, Bob! 우리가 이 경기장에서 다시 만나리라고 생각했어요.
   Hello, Mr. Bob! I thought (that) we would meet again in this stadium.

B: 나도 그랬어요. 우리는 이 경기를 전에도 놓치지 않았어요, 그렇죠?
   So did I. We have never missed this match before, have we?

A: 당신은 어느 팀이 이길 거라고 생각합니까?
   Which team do you think will win?

B: 오, 아무도 모르죠. Dodgers 팀은 투수가 훌륭하고 반면에 Giants는 타자가 강해요.
   Oh, God knows, the Dodgers have fine pitchers while the Giants have strong hitters.

A: 봐요! 첫 번째 투구가 옵니다.
   Look! Here comes the first pitch.

B: 그것은 볼이네요. 너무 높았네요.
   That is a ball. Too high.

A: 몇 회 경기를 하고 있습니까?
   What inning are they playing now?

B: 그들은 8회 말 경기를 하고 있어요.
   They are playing in the bottom of the eighth inning.

cf) in the top of(the first(upper) half of)

A: 스코어가 몇이죠?
What's the score?

B: 스코어는 2대 1로 Dodgers 팀이 이기고 있어요.
The score is 2 to 1, the Dodgers' favor(in favor of the Dodgers).

A: 타자가 누구죠?
Who is at bat?

B: 3번 타자 Greg Maddux예요.
The third batter Greg Maddux.

A: 훌륭한 타자입니까?
Is he a good batter?

B: 예, 그는 가끔 홈런을 쳐요.
Yes, he often whacks out[2] a homer.

---

2) whacks out; 홈런을 치다. 강하게 치다

III. Sports Activities

Learning Terms

base-loaded homer
batting order
edge: The Tigers edged out the Lions 5-4.
force out / shut out
infield / outfield
pitcher / catcher / hitter / batter / runner
right fielder / left fielder / center fielder
sac(rifice) bunt / squeeze bunt
squeeze

"Hitting is timing. Pitching is upsetting timing."
- Warren Spahn (former pitcher in major league)

III. Sports Activities

Winning Is Not Everything

The world of sports is full of both dramatic victories and heart breaking defeats. Players constantly try to be fitter, stronger, and faster, performing their hardest for the masses of cheering spectators who come to support their favorite teams or players. It seems that their ultimate goal is to win. However, it's important to remember that some of the greatest moments in sports have nothing to do with wins or losses. The following story illustrates how good sportsmanship can touch our hearts more than a goal or a home run ever could.

Sara Tucholsky was a softball player for Western Oregon University in the United States. In 2008, while her team was playing against a rival school, a play of sportsmanship took place that attracted admiration from people all around the world.

In the second inning, Tucholsky hit the first home run of her career. As she watched the ball soar through the air, she mistakenly forgot to step on first base. Realizing her error, she stopped short and quickly turned to touch the base. Unfortunately, her right knee gave out[3], causing her to fall to the ground. She managed to crawl back to first base but was in too much pain to go any further.

The umpire explained that the rule prohibited any of Sara's teammates from helping her around the bases. A new player could take Sara's place, but the hit would be ruled a single rather than a home run.

While the Western Oregon coaches and players tried to decide what

---

3) give out: to come to an end; to be used up; 끝장나다

III. Sports Activities

to do, the first baseman from the other team, Mallory Holtman, made a surprising request. In a show of great sportsmanship, she found a solution for her opponent. Mallory asked the umpire if she and her teammate could help Sara around the bases.

The umpire thought for a while and decided that there was no rule against it. So Mallory and her team mate, Liz Wallace, carefully lifted Sara from the ground. Supporting her in their arms, they slowly made their way around the bases, allowing her to touch each base with her good leg.

"Thank you so much," Sara said with tears in her eyes. By the time they reached second base, the three young women were laughing together. But the crowd wasn't laughing. The sight of the two women carrying a player from the opposing team lifted the spectators' hearts, and they rose up to give the trio a big hand as they crossed home plate.

Sara's team won the game 4 to 2, ending any chances (Mallory's team had) of making the playoffs. But that didn't bother Mallory. "In the end, it's not about winning and losing so much," she said. "It was about this girl. She hit it over the fence and was in pain, and she deserved a home run." By helping Sara touch home plate, Mallory and Liz touched the hearts[4] of millions of people.

---

4) touch the hearts: 감동을 주다

3. Swimming

Actual Scene

A: 지금은 수영의 계절이야, 그렇지 않니?
   Now is the season for swimming, isn't it?

B: 그래, 나는 매일 수영을 해.
   Yes, I swim everyday.

A: 너도? 어쩐지 너 햇볕에 많이 탔더라. 수영 잘 하니?
   Do you? No wonder you've got so sunburnt. Can you swim well?

B: 아니, 조금. 너는?
   No, just a little. And you?

A: 나는 소위 말하는 맥주병이야.
   I am what we call a 'hammer'.

B: 그게 수영 스트로크를 한 번도 못하는 사람들에게 주어진 별명이니?
   Is it a nickname given to those who cannot swim a single stroke?

A: 응, 그래.
   Yes, it is.

B: 난 지난 여름까지는 맥주병이었어(수영을 전혀 못했어).
   I was a 'hammer' myself till last summer.

A: 어떻게 수영을 배웠니?
   How did you learn to swim?

B: 우리 학교의 모든 학생들은 학기말 시험이 끝난 직후에 수영수업에 참가

III. Sports Activities

하게 돼 있어.

All the students of our school are supposed to attend swimming lessons soon after the final exam is over.

A: 수업을 며칠간 하는데?

How many days do you have lessons?

B: 일주일 동안.

For a week.

A: 일주일이면 네가 수영을 배우는데 충분하니?

Is only a week enough for you to learn swimming?

B: 충분해. 선생님들이 초보자들을 특별히 돌봐주시거든.

Quite enough. The teachers take special care of beginners.

A: 넌 어떤 영법을 가장 좋아하니?

What style of swimming do you like best?

B: 난 크롤 스트로크를 가장 좋아해.

I like the crawl stroke best.

III. Sports Activities

Learning Terms

breast stroke / butterfly / free style
flip turn
laptime
long distance swim
spring board
swimming suit
swim like a fish(rock)

"Seventy-five percent of our planet is water - can you swim?"
- Author Unknown

III. Sports Activities

Swimming

The aquatic sport of swimming is based on the human act of swimming. There are also swimming competitions for endurance or precedence rather than speed, such as crossing the English Channel or other stretches of open water.

Swimming is distinguished from other aquatic sports(such as diving, synchronized swimming and water polo) that involve swimming but the goal is neither speed nor endurance.

History

Competitive swimming in Europe started around 1800, mostly using the breaststroke. In 1873, after copying the front crawl used by Native Americans, John Arthur Trudgen introduced the trudgen[5] to Western swimming competitions. Due to a British disregard for splashing, Trudgen employed a scissor kick instead of the front crawl's flutter kick.

Swimming was part of the first modern Olympic games in 1896 in Athens. In 1902 Richard Cavill introduced the front crawl to the Western world. In 1908, the world swimming association, Fédération Internationale de Natation (FINA), was formed.

---

5) trudgen; 트루전 영법

Modalities

Butterfly

Butterfly(a.k.a. fly) is a stroke in which the swimmer brings both hands over their head close to the water, breathing forward. When turning, all walls must be touched with two hands at the same time and the swimmer will be disqualified if his/her arms do not clear the water[6] at the same time.

Backstroke

Backstroke(a.k.a. back) is a stroke which is similar to the front crawl, except on your back. Kicking by alternating both feet, pulling each arm one at a time, and looking straight up. At walls, flip turns are permitted(the swimmer is to turn on to his/her front before performing the turn), and a two-hand touch is not necessary.

Breaststroke

Breaststroke(a.k.a. breast) is a stroke where the swimmer kicks legs out(much like a frog, but more whip like, it is important to keep the kick narrow), scoops the water in towards the chest with his or her hands and then thrusts the hands out in front just before the kick is repeated.

One underwater 'pull-out' is permitted for the start and after every wall with a streamline glide, one breaststroke leg kick and one pull to the surface. Each wall requires a two-hand(simultaneous) touch.

---

6) clear the water: 물 밖으로 나오다

III. Sports Activities

4. Basketball

Actual Scene

A: Bob, 너 오늘 경기 잘 했다. 너의 점프슛이 아주 좋아.

You played well in the game today, Mr. Bob. Your jumpshot is quite good.

B: 고마워. 그 프리드로우를 놓쳤다는 게 믿기지 않아. 눈 감고도 프리드로우를 할 수 있는데!

Thanks. I can't believe (that) I missed that free throw! I can make those with my eyes closed!

A: 심판이 너의 팔을 잡은 사람에게 파울을 불어줘서 좋았어. 어쨌든, 그는 좋은 선수가 아니었어.

I'm glad the ref[7] called a foul on that man who grabbed your arm. He wasn't a very good player, anyway.

B: 알아. 드리블링을 하지 않고 워킹(트래블링)을 했어. 심판이 그 사람에게 워킹을 선언하지 않은 것을 믿을 수 없어.

I know. He was traveling instead of dribbling. I can't believe the ref didn't call him on that.

A: 어~있잖아, 네가 프리드로우를 놓쳤지만, 3점 슛을 잘 했잖아.

You know, even though you missed that free throw, you did make a good three-point shot.

B: 응, 그게 좋았어. 그게 내가 놓친 슛을 보상해주었다고 생각해.

Yeah, that was good. I guess that made up for the shot I missed.

---

7) ref: referee 주심

III. Sports Activities

A: 놀리는 거니? 그래서 너의 팀이 이긴 거야! 진심이야, Bob아. 정말 잘 했어.
Are you kidding? That's the reason your team won the game! I mean it, Bob. You're really good.

B: 어, 그렇게 생각하니? 그래, 1대 1 경기 좀 하러 갈래?
Think so, huh? So, you wanna go play a little one-on-one?

III. Sports Activities

Learning Terms

court / backcourt
field goal / free throw
jumpshot
travel / drive
dribble
one-on-one
personal foul / technical foul / team foul
give up the body

"The invention of basketball was not an accident. It was developed to meet a need. Those boys simply would not play Drop the Handkerchief."
- Dr. James Naismith (The Basketball Inventor)

III. Sports Activities

Win the Game

Within the crowded gymnasium, Kenmore and Taft were playing a hard-fought game[8] for the city basketball championship. Ted Shannon, left forward for Kenmore, caught a high forward pass. He wanted to pass to Billy Stern, but Billy was unable to break loose from his guard.

The Kenmore crowd shouted, "Shoot, Ted! Take a chance!"

It was a difficult shot, from almost the middle of the court. But, Ted took a chance. The ball rose in a high arc, struck against a backboard, hit the ring, hesitated, and then dropped through the basket.

Above the wild cheering from the Kenmore rooters, the referee's whistle sounded. He called, "Time out for Taft!"

The Kenmore team was still in the game, but there was less than a minute to play. Taft was leading, 33 to 32. Was it too late? Could they win?

Two things Ted wanted more than anything else. First, he wanted Kenmore to win the city championship. Second, he wanted to win the silver cup that the Times-Citizen newspaper was offering to the player that scored the most points during that season.

Ted had done all that he could to get himself ready for the game. He had practiced hard. He had been very careful about his diet. He had especially tried to eat foods rich in vitamins to keep himself healthy, alert, and growing.

Art Clark, manager of the Kenmore team, said, "Ted, you and Billy

---

8) hard-fought game: 힘든 경기

III. Sports Activities

are tied. That's the way you'll finish unless one of you score in the last minute of play."

As Billy came over, Art said, "I was just telling Ted that you two fellows are tied for high scoring."

"Right now I don't care about scoring the most points — or the cup," Billy answered. "What I want is to win the game!"

Again the whistle sounded. The game was on. Taft took the ball, working it down the court, while their fans roared approval. Almost under the Kenmore basket, the Taft center grabbed a pass from one of their forwards. Then he dodged away from the Kenmore guard. He was ready to shoot, when Ted hurled himself at him, and the ball dropped free[9].

When it was scooped by another Kenmore player, their crowd yelled, "Come on, Kenmore! We want another basket!" There was only half a minute left, as Ted leaped high and took a quick pass from Billy. Then he threw the ball to Lew and raced to the right.

Lew tried but failed. The Kenmore crowd groaned. Billy caught the ball, but, as he was about to shoot, one of the Taft guards blocked him. He ducked and whipped the ball outward in a hard, underhand pass. "Ted," Billy yelled. "Shoot!"

The ball hit Ted's outstretched hands. He was all alone on the right-hand side of the court, well out from the basket. It would be another difficult shot. Could he do it again?

While the Taft center charged at him, Ted took careful aim. This was

---

9) 볼이 떨어져 누구에게도 속하지 않다

his big moment. A basket now would not only win the game, but give him the silver cup!

Suddenly everything changed. Out of the corner of his eye, he saw Billy almost under the basket and no one was near him! Billy's words flashed through Ted's mind. "Right now I don't care about scoring the most points — or the cup, either. What I want is to win the game!"

"Win the game," Ted thought. That was the important thing. Never mind the most points. Win the game! Take no chances on a difficult shot….

The Taft guard and center were almost upon him when he passed the ball to Billy. Billy aimed. The ball fell through the basket!

The whistle blew. The game was over. Kenmore had won the championship!

In the locker-room, Captain Goldman came to the bench where Ted and Billy were dressing. "That was a big thing you did, Ted," he said. "That's what I call being a good sport[10]."

Ted shrugged. "Billy would have done the same thing in my place, wouldn't you Billy?" "I'm not sure," Billy admitted "I hope I would have been that good a sport. That was tough for you, Ted, missing out like that on high-scoring honors. It's almost as if you handed the thing to me."

Ted grinned. "Right now I don't care so much about that — or the cup, either. All I wanted was to win the game."

---

10) 좋은 녀석

III. Sports Activities

5. Volleyball

Actual Scene

A: 이번 주말에 배구 좀 하고 싶니? 친구 몇 명과 내가 함께 모여서 토요일마다 경기를 하려고 해.

Do you want to play some volleyball this weekend? Several friends and I like to get together and play on Saturdays.

B: 그래, 그러나 말해 두는데 경기를 잘 못해. 어쨌든 너처럼 잘 못해.

Sure, but I warn you that I don't play very well. Not like you, anyway.

A: 무슨 말 하는 거야? Bob, 너는 킬러 스파이크가 있잖아. 그리고 훌륭한 세터 잖아.

What are you talking about? Bob, you have a killer spike, and you're a good setter.

B: 그럴지 몰라, 그러나 반은 네트볼을 쳐. 나는 네가 스파이크하는 방법이 좋아 – 아무도 리턴하지 못 하잖아.

Maybe so, but half the time I hit net balls. I like the way you kill the ball - no one can return it.

A: 나는 또한 딩크샷을 좋아해. 사람들이 내가 스파이크할 것으로 생각해, 그런데 그라운드에 살짝 떨어지지.

I also like to dink it. People think I'm going to spike, and then it just drops to the ground.

B: 너가 알다시피 내가 경기를 하면 우리 팀이 사이드아웃을 많이 할 거야, 그렇지 않니? 확실히 우리 팀을 할 거야?

You know my team will have lots of side outs if I play, don't you? Are

III. Sports Activities

you sure you want to be on my team?

A: 그렇게 우리가 로테이션을 해, 그래서 모두가 서브 기회를 갖는 거야. 어쨌든 재미로 하니까 걱정하지 마.

That's the way we rotate, so everyone gets a chance to serve. We just play for fun, anyway, so don't worry about it.

B: 좋아, 나도 끼워 줘.

Okay, count me in.

III. Sports Activities

Learning Terms

spike / block
decoy attack / approach attack / back attack
dink the ball
kill the ball
netball
setter
side out
spike
toss

"Volleyball is the sport through which I am able to express my God-given talents of being an athlete."
- Author Unknown

III. Sports Activities

Volleyball

Volleyball is an Olympic team sport in which two teams of 6 players are separated by a net. Each team tries to score points by grounding a ball on the other team's court under organized rules.

This article focuses on competitive indoor volleyball; numerous other variations of volleyball have developed, most notably the Olympic spin-off sport beach volleyball.

The complete rules are extensive. But simply, play proceeds as follows: A player on one of the teams begins a rally by serving the ball(tossing or releasing it and then hitting it with a hand or arm), from behind the back boundary line of the court, over the net, and into the receiving team's court. The receiving team must not let the ball be grounded within their court.

They may touch the ball as many as three times. Typically, the first two touches to set up for an attack, an attempt to direct the ball back over the net in such a way that the serving team is unable to prevent it.

The rally continues, with each team allowed as many as three consecutive touches, until either (1): a team makes a kill, grounding the ball on the opponent's court and winning the rally; or (2): a team commits a fault and loses the rally.

The team that wins the rally is awarded a point, and serves the ball to start the next rally. A few of the most common faults include: causing the ball to touch the ground outside the opponents' court; catching and throwing the ball; double hitting: two consecutive contacts with the ball

III. Sports Activities

made by the same player; four consecutive contacts with the ball made by the same team. The ball is usually played with the hands or arms, but players can legally strike or push(short contact) the ball with any part of the body.

A number of consistent techniques have evolved in volleyball, including spiking and blocking(because these plays are made above the top of the net. The vertical jump is an athletic skill emphasized in the sport) as well as passing, setting, specialized player positions and offensive and defensive structures.

6. Soccer

Actual Scene

A: 누가 경기 진영을 정할 거죠(토스를 할 거죠)?
   Who is going to make the call[11]?

B: 팀의 주장으로서 제가 앞면인지 뒷면인지 콜 하겠습니다.
   As a team captain, I'll call heads or tails[12].

A: 좋아요, 그럼 이제 동전던지기를 합시다.
   Okay, then it's time to flip the coin.

B: 제가 앞면으로 하죠.
   I think I'm going to call heads.

A: 경기시작 개시를 할 시간이네요.
   It's time for the opening kickoff.

B: 오늘 우리 팀 경기 어떨 거 같니?
   How do you think we're going to play today?

A: 이번 시합은 별로 느낌이 좋지 않은데.
   I'm not feeling so good about this game.

B: 나도 그래. 우리 팀이 좀 힘들 것 같은 생각이 들어.
   Me too. I think we're going to have a tough time.

---

11) make the call; 진영을 정하다. 출석을 부르다. 토스를 하다.
12) heads or tails; 동전의 앞면과 뒷면

Ⅲ. Sports Activities

Learning Terms

Association football
Soccer
Football
Knock out competition(=tournament)
Qualifying
Quarterfinal
Final

There is no such thing as endless winner in the sports world.
- Author Unknown

History

'Association football' is the official name of the game. It is referred to as 'football' or 'soccer' in some countries, derived from the 'soc' in 'association.' It is believed to have originated from a simple ball passing game played in Ancient Greece in 7~6 B.C. with a ball called 'episkyros,' while some say that a similar game was played in Ancient China even before then. The game spread widely throughout the military and was introduced in England by Roman soldiers. This game, called 'harpastum' is believed to be the origin of football in England. Football became more structured and began to spread to other parts of the world via foreigners who would take it back to their home countries or via ministers, missionaries, soldiers and merchants. With its growing popularity, the international football body FIFA(International Federation of Association Football) was formed in 1904 and currently has over 200 member countries. Football has been included on the programme of the Olympic Games since 1900, and other international football events include World Cup, Women's World Cup, and U-20 World Cup.

Football was introduced in Korea by the crew of the British Royal Navy ship 'Flying Horse', which landed at Incheon port in 1882 during the 19th year of King Gojong's reign. It began to spread widely when a government school in Seoul included the sport on their curriculum in 1904.

It began to take form of an official competitive sport with proper equipments under standard international rules in 1920s. The first official

III. Sports Activities

football game was held in 1921 and the Korean Football Association was established on May 22, 1928, laying the foundation for the spread and development of soccer in Korea. KFA closed its doors towards the end of[13] the Japanese colonization and reopened on September 4, 1948. Korea also became a member of FIFA the same year and also joined the Asian Football Confederation in 1954.

Football is a sport played between two teams of eleven players, and it is one of the world's most popular sports. The game is played on a rectangular[14] field of grass or green artificial turf, with a goal in the middle of each of the short ends. The objective of the game is to score by driving the ball into the opposing goal. The goal keepers are the only players allowed to touch the ball with their hands or arms, while the field players typically use their feet to kick the ball.

Rules

In football, eleven players form one team and try to score points by driving the ball into the opposing team's goal. Only goal keepers are allowed to touch the ball with their hands from inside the penalty area. Field players use their hands only for throw-in of the game ball which has been carried out of play, and use their feet, head, or torso to maneuver the ball.

Qualification round and knockout competition

---

13) towards the end of; ~말 경에
14) rectangular; 직사각형의

III. Sports Activities

In the event of a tie, only final match goes into overtime and all other games go into penalty shootout. If final match results in a tie, game goes into overtime consisting of two 15 minutes, game goes into penalty shootout if scores are level after overtime. Match consists of two halves of 45 minutes each, with 15 minutes halftime break in between.

FIFA World Cup

The history of world cup begins in 1928, when FIFA president and French Jules Rimet decided to stage an international football tournament. The inaugural[15] edition, held in Uruguay in 1930, was contested as a final tournament of only 13 teams invited by the organization. Since then, the FIFA World Cup has experienced successive expansions and format remodeling to its current 32-team final tournament preceded by a two-year qualifying process, involving almost 200 teams from all over the world.

The world's first international football match was a challenge match played in Glasgow in 1872 between Scotland and England, which ended in a 0–0 draw. The first international tournament, the inaugural edition of the British Home Championship, took place in 1884.

As football grew in popularity in other parts of the world at the turn[16] of the 20th century, it was held as a demonstration sport with no medals awarded at the 1900 and 1904 Summer Olympics, however, the IOC has retroactively[17] upgraded their

---

15) inaugural; 취임의, 최초의, 제1회의
16) at the turn of; 전환기에

III. Sports Activities

status to official events, and at the 1906 Intercalated[18] Games.

At the 1908 Summer Olympics in London, football became an official competition. After FIFA was founded in 1904, it tried to arrange an international football tournament between nations outside the Olympic framework in Switzerland in 1906. Thes;e were very early days for international football, and the official history of FIFA describes the competition as having been a failure.

The 2014 FIFA World Cup is the 20th FIFA World Cup, an international men's football tournament that is currently taking place in Brazil. Brazil was elected unchallenged as host nation in 2007 after the international football federation, FIFA, decreed that the tournament would be staged in South America for the first time since 1978 in Argentina, and the fifth time overall.

The FIFA World Cup, often simply the World Cup, is an international association football competition contested by the senior men's national teams of the members of FIFA, the sport's global governing body. The championship has been awarded every four years since the inaugural tournament in 1930, except in 1942 and 1946 when it was not held because of the Second World War. The current champions are Spain, who won the 2010 tournament in South Africa.

The current format of the tournament involves 32 teams competing for the title at venues within the host nation(s) over a period of about a month; this phase is often called the World Cup Finals. A qualification

---

17) retroactively; 소급적으로, 역행적으로
18) intercalate; ~ 삽입하다, 윤으로 하다

phase, which currently takes place over the preceding three years, is used to determine which teams qualify for the tournament together with the host nation(s).

The World Cup is the most widely viewed and followed sporting event in the world, exceeding even the Olympic Games; the cumulative[19] audience of all matches of the 2006 FIFA World Cup was estimated to be 26.29 billion with an estimated 715.1 million people watching the final match, a ninth of the entire population of the planet. The next three World Cups will be hosted by Russia in 2018, and Qatar in 2022.

The 2014 FIFA World Cup

The 2014 FIFA World Cup was the 20th FIFA World Cup, the tournament for the association football world championship, which took place at several venues across Brazil. Germany won the tournament, defeating runner-up Argentina 1-0 in the final match.

It began on 12 June, with a group stage, and concluded on 13 July with the championship match. It was the second time that Brazil has hosted the competition, the first being in 1950. Brazil was elected unchallenged as host nation in 2007 after the international football federation, FIFA, decreed[20] that the tournament would be staged in South America for the first time since 1978 in Argentina, and the fifth time overall.

The national teams of 31 countries advanced through qualification competitions that began in June 2011 to participate with the host nation

---

19) cumulative; 누적의
20) decree; ~을 (법령에 의거하여) 명하다, 선언하다; […인 것으로] 정하다, 명하다

III. Sports Activities

Brazil in the final tournament. A total of 64 matches were being played in 12 cities across Brazil in either new or redeveloped stadiums. For the first time at a World Cup finals, match officials used goal-line technology, as well as vanishing foam[21] for free kicks.

All world champion teams since the first World Cup in 1930 – Argentina, Brazil, England, France, Germany, Italy, Spain and Uruguay – qualified for this competition. The title holders, Spain, were eliminated at the group stage, along with previous winners England and Italy. Uruguay was eliminated in the Round of 16 and France was eliminated at the quarterfinals. In the final between two former champions Argentina and Germany won the title by defeating Argentina after extra time, thus becoming the first European team to win a World Cup in the Americas. This result marked the first time that sides from the same continent had won three successive World Cups(following Italy in 2006 and Spain in 2010).

As the winners, Germany qualified for the 2017 FIFA Confederations Cup. During the 2014 FIFA World Cup, the FIFA Fan Fest in the host cities received 5 million people, and the country received 1 million foreigners from 202 countries.

---

21) vanishing foam;~ 뿌려서 마크하는 사라지는 거품, vanishing spray

7. American Football

Actual Scene

A: 여기 맥주요. 샌드위치는 곧 될 겁니다. 제가 킥오프를 놓쳤나요?

Here's the beer, the sandwiches will be ready soon. Have I missed the kickoff?

B: 아닙니다, 막 시작하려 합니다. Favre는 정말로 훌륭한 쿼터백입니다. 나는 그가 이 경기를 잘 하기를 바랍니다.

Nope, it's just about to happen. Favre is sure a good quarterback. I hope he plays well this game.

A: 지난 번 경기를 잘 했습니다. 그는 전 경기 동안 멋진 스파이어럴 패스를 던졌어요.

He did during the last game. He threw beautiful spiral passes the whole game.

B: 예, 그러나 우리 선수들이 계속 태클을 받았어요. 우리가 오늘 이 팀을 이기려면 터치다운을 많이 해야 해요.

Yes, but our players kept getting tackled. We need a lot of touchdowns to beat this team today.

A: 선수들이 오른 쪽 엔드존에서 터치다운을 하는 한!

As long as the players make the touchdowns in the right endzone!

B: 예, 저 선수가 자책 스코어를 한 경기를 기억하나요?

Yeah, remember the game when that player scored against his own team?

A: 확실히 기억하지요! 그의 팀은 그에게 정말로 화났어요. 오, 시작하네요.

III. Sports Activities

I sure do! His team was really mad at him. Oh, here we go.

B: 멋진 킥오프입니다! 우리 팀이 벌써 볼을 갖고 달려가고 있네요. 어, 그 샌드위치는 어떻게 되었나?

Beautiful kickoff! Our team's already got the ball and is running with it. Say, how about those sandwiches?

III. Sports Activities

Learning Terms

kickoff

quarterback / guard / offensive linemen / running back / wide receiver

spiral

tackle

touchdown

endzone

scoring

"Pro football is like nuclear warfare. There are no winners, only survivors."
- Frank Gifford

III. Sports Activities

American College Football Rules

American football grew out of the English game of rugby. Unlike soccer, the foot hardly ever touches the ball in American football.(Soccer is the game most of the world calls football.)

The Field is 100 yards long(and 160 feet wide). The middle of the field is the 50 yard line. The lines are labeled every 10 yards descending in both directions from the 50 yard line. Thus there are two 40 yard lines and no 60 yard line. Each team owns half of the field(they switch sides every 15 minutes of play). Thus, the two 40 yard lines are distinguished by who owns them. The 'zero yard line' is called the goal line. The areas to either side of those 100 yards, extending 10 yards past the goal lines, are called the end zones.

Teams try to get the ball past the opponent's goal line into the end zone to score a touchdown. At the far edge of each endzone are the goal posts which, together with the cross bar, looks like a big H. These are used only when a team decides to kick a field goal instead of going for a touchdown or to kick for an extra point after scoring a touchdown. To score the field goal or extra point, the ball must go between the vertical posts and over the bar.

Kickoffs: At the start of the game there is a coin toss to see which team gets the ball first. The team that has the ball is the offense; the other team is the defense. A football game is supposedly one hour, but takes about three hours to play because the clock is often stopped for various reasons. The game is divided into 15 minute quarters with a major division at 30 minutes which is called half time. At the end of the first and third quarters, the players switch sides.

The ball is moved to the corresponding point on the other side of the field, and play continues. This switching of sides evens up any advantage due to the sun or wind. The players leave the field for 20 minutes at half-time. After half-time, play does not continue where it ended. Instead, the team that originally lost the coin toss gets to have the ball first following another kickoff.

Scoring: The object of the game is to score more points than your opponent. A touchdown is worth 6 points. After a touchdown, the team then attempts to kick the ball through the goal posts to get an extra point. Because this kick almost always works, most people think of a touchdown as being worth 7 points and then subtract a point if the extra point kick is missed.

The team that scored the touchdown has the option of trying to get the ball into the opponent's end zone again in just one running or passing play instead of kicking for the extra point. If this conversion[22] works, they get two points instead of just one. This is, however, more than twice as difficult as kicking an extra point. A field goal is worth 3 points.

---

22) conversion: 전환, 개조, 트라이 이후 추가 득점(하기)

8. Camping

Actual Scene

A: 여보게! 어디 갔다 왔어?
   Hello! Where have you been?

B: 제주도에서 막 돌아왔어.
   I've just come back from Jeju Island.

A: 오, 그래? 뭐 하러 갔는데?
   Oh, have you? What did you go there for?

B: 급우들 몇 명과 캠핑 갔어.
   I went camping with some of my classmates.

A: 캠핑? 참 즐거웠겠는데!
   Camping? How happy you must have been!

B: 응, 좋았어. 우리는 지난 금요일 오후 7시에 부산을 출발해 다음날 아침 7시에 거기에 도착했어.
   Yes, it was wonderful. We left Busan at 7 p.m. last Friday and arrived there at 7 a.m. the next morning.

캠핑지가 그 섬의 서해안 바닷가에 위치해 있어.
The camping ground is located on the beach in the western coast of the island.

그 뒤에 있는 언덕 꼭대기로부터 황해를 볼 수 있어. 그리고 반대편에는 우리나라에서 두 번째로 높은 한라산이 있어. 캠핑하기에 좋은(멋진) 곳이야.
From the top of a hill behind it, we can see the Yellow Sea, and on the other side, Mt. Halla, the second highest mountain in our country. It's a

delightful place for camping.

A: 캠핑하는 동안 뭐가 가장 인상적이었어?
What impressed you most during the camp life?

B: 별이 빛나는 하늘 아래 캠프파이어에 둘러 앉아 이야기 나눈 것. 인생에서 좋은 추억이 될 거야.
A talking around the camp fire under the starry sky. It will remain a good memory through my life.

III. Sports Activities

Learning Terms

canteen; mess tin
camping village
camping outfit
subsidiary food

"Camping: The art of getting closer to nature while getting farther away from the nearest cold beverage, hot shower and flush toilet."
- Author Unknown

Camping

Camping is an outdoor recreational activity. The participants, known as campers, leave urban areas, their home region, or civilization and enjoy nature while spending one or several nights, usually at a campsite, which may have cabins. Camping may involve the use of a tent, a primitive structure, or no shelter at all.

Camping as a recreational activity became popular in the early 20th century. Campers frequent national parks, other publicly owned natural areas, and privately owned campgrounds.

Camping is also used as a cheap form of accommodation for people attending large open air events such as sporting meetings and music festivals. Organizers usually provide a field and basic amenities.

Definition

Camping describes a range of activities. Survivalist campers set off with little more than their boots, whereas recreational vehicle travelers arrive equipped with their own electricity, heat, and patio furniture.

Camping is often enjoyed in conjunction with activities, such as: hiking, hill walking, climbing, canoeing, mountain biking, motorcycling, swimming, and fishing. Camping may be combined with hiking either as backpacking or as a series of day hikes from a central location.

Some people vacation in permanent camps with cabins and other facilities(such as hunting camps or children's summer camps), but a stay at such a camp is usually not considered 'camping'.

III. Sports Activities

The term camping(or camping out) may also be applied to those who live outdoors, out of necessity(as in the case of the homeless), or for people waiting overnight in queues. It does not, however, apply to cultures whose technology does not include sophisticated dwellings. Camping may be referred to colloquially as roughing it[23].

Range of amenities

Campers span a broad range of age, ability and ruggedness, campsites are designed in many ways as well. Many campgrounds have sites with facilities such as fire rings, barbecue grills, utilities, shared bathrooms and laundry, as well as close access to recreational facilities. Not all campsites have similar levels of development. Campsites can range from a patch of dirt, to a level, paved pad with sewer and electricity. For more information on facilities, see the campsite and RV(Recreation Vehicle) park articles.

---

23) roughing it ; (잠깐 동안) 불편한 생활을 하다

9. Tennis

Actual Scene

A: Smith, 넌 재미삼아 뭘 하니?

　　Smith, what do you do for fun?

B: 글쎄, 나는 보통 방과 후에 친구들과 테니스를 해.

　　Well, I usually play tennis with my classmates after school.

A: 그러면, 너는 테니스 잘 하지, 그렇지 않니?

　　Then, you are good at it, aren't you?

B: 오, 아니. 나는 테니스를 좋아하지만, 잘 못해. 너는?

　　Oh, no. I'm very fond of it, but a very poor hand at it. And you?

A: 나도 그래.

　　So am I.

B: 그러면, 이제 우리 한 게임 할까?

　　Then, shall we have a game now?

A: 좋아.

　　All right.

B: 우리 단식을 할까, 복식을 할까?

　　Shall we play singles or doubles?

A: 단식 먼저 하자.

　　Let's play singles first.

B: 우리 몇 세트의 게임을 할까?

III. Sports Activities

How many sets of games shall we have?

A: 3세트 게임을 하자.

Let's have a game of three sets.

B: 누가 심판을 하지?

Who will be the umpire?

A: 밥에게 심판해달라고 할게. 밥, 우리를 위해 심판 좀 해 줄래?

I'll ask Bob to act as our umpire. Bob, will you please act as umpire for us?

C: 응, 기꺼이.

Yes, with pleasure.

B: 밥, 연습 시간 좀 갖자, 그럴 거야?

Bob, please let's have a little time for practice, will you?

C: 좋아.

O. K.

III. Sports Activities

Learning Terms

continental grip / eastern grip / western grip

double fault

love: a loan word from French word 'l'oueff' / deuce

smash / volley / lobbing

forehand stroke / backhand stroke

up-player / back-player

play forward / play back

"My great strength is that I have no weaknesses."
- John McEnroe

III. Sports Activities

Tennis

Tennis is a sport usually played between two players (singles) or between two teams of two players each(doubles). Each player uses a racket that is strung to strike a hollow[24] rubber ball covered with felt[25] past a net into the opponent's court.

The modern game of tennis originated in the United Kingdom in the late 19th century as 'lawn tennis' which has heavy connections to various field/lawn games as well as to the ancient game of real tennis. After its creation, tennis spread throughout the upper-class English-speaking population before spreading around the world. Tennis is an Olympic sport and is played at all levels of society at all ages. The sport can be played by anyone who can hold a racket, including people in wheelchairs.

The rules of tennis have not changed much since the 1890s. Two exceptions are that from 1908 to 1960 the server had to keep one foot on the ground at all times, and then the adoption of the tie-break in the 1970s. A recent addition to professional tennis has been the adoption of electronic review technology coupled with[26] a point challenge system, which allows a player to challenge the line(or chair) umpire's call of a point.

Tennis enjoys millions of recreational players and is also a hugely

---

24) hollow; 속이 비어있는

25) felt; 융단, 펠트(모직이나 털을 압축해서 만든 부드럽고 두꺼운 천)

26) coupled with; …와 결부된, 연관된

popular worldwide spectator sport, especially the four Grand Slam tournaments(also referred to as the 'Majors'): the Australian Open, the French Open, Wimbledon, and the US Open.

Scoring

A tennis match is determined through the best of 3 or $5^{27)}$ sets. Typically for both men's and women's matches, the first player to win two sets wins the match. At certain important tennis tournaments for men, including all four Grand Slam tournaments and the final of the Olympic Games, the first man to win three sets wins the match. A set consists of games, and games, in turn, consist of points.

A game consists of a sequence of points played with the same player serving. A game is won by the first player to have won at least four points in total and at least two points more than the opponent. The running score of each game is described in a manner peculiar to tennis: scores from zero to three points are described as 'love', 'fifteen', 'thirty', and 'forty', respectively.

If at least three points have been scored by each player, and the scores are equal, the score is 'deuce'. If at least three points have been scored by each side and a player has one more point than his opponent, the score of the game is 'advantage' for the player in the lead. During informal games, 'advantage' can also be called 'ad in' or 'ad out', depending on whether the serving player or receiving player is ahead, respectively.

---

27) 3판 2승 또는 5판 3승

10. Mountaineering

Actual Scene

A: 여보게, Bob! 본 지 오랜만이다. 잘 지내니?

　　Hello, Bob! It's been ages since I saw you last. Are you well?

B: 응, 잘 지내. 고마워.

　　Yes, very fine, thank you.

A: 방학 중에 어디 갔니?

　　Did you go anywhere during the vacation?

B: 응, 7월말에 내 사촌들과 지리산에 갔어.

　　Yes, I went to Mt. Jiri with my cousins at the end of July.

A: 여행이 즐거웠니?

　　Did you enjoy the trip?

B: 응, 매유 유쾌했어, 거기에 처음이었기에 내가 보고 들은 모든 것이 흥미로 웠어.

　　Yes, it was very pleasant. As it was my first visit there, everything I saw and heard was interesting to me.

A: (너의) 여행에 대해 이야기해 줘.

　　Tell me about your trip, please.

B: 우리는 순천에서 버스로 구례로 출발했어.

　　We started from Suncheon by bus for Gurye.

A: 버스가 붐볐니?

　　Was the bus crowded?

B: 관광객과 하이커들로 꽉 찼지만, 운 좋게도 좌석을 차지할 수 있었어.
It was full of tourists and hikers, but fortunately we could find seats.

III. Sports Activities

Learning Terms

mountaineer / alpinist / mountain climber / hiker / trekker
pick-axe
rock climbing
rucksack / backpack
mountaineering boots
seil / rope

"One does not climb to attain enlightenment, rather one climbs because he is enlightened."
- Zen Master Futomaki

Mountaineering

Mountaineering or mountain climbing is the sport, hobby or profession[28] of walking, hiking, backpacking and climbing mountains.

In Europe it is also referred to as alpinism, while in the Americas the term refers to a particular style of mountain climbing, that involves a mixture of ice climbing, and rock climbing. The climbers carry all their gear with them at all times. In the Himalayan regions the style of mountaineering is Expedition.

While mountaineering began as attempts to reach the highest point of unclimbed mountains, it has branched into specializations that address different aspects of the mountain and consists of three areas: rock-craft, snow-craft and skiing, depending on whether the route chosen is over rock, snow or ice. All require experience, athletic ability, and technical knowledge or maintaining safety.

The UIAA or Union Internationale des Associations d'Alpinisme is the world governing body in mountaineering and climbing, addressing issues like Access, Medical, Mountain Protection, Safety, Youth and Ice Climbing.

Technique

Snow

Compacted snow conditions allow mountaineers to progress on foot.

---

28) (특히 많은 교육이 필요한 전문적인) 직업

Frequently crampons are required to travel efficiently over snow and ice. Crampons have 8-14 spikes and are attached to a mountaineer's boots. They are used on hard snow(neve[29]) and ice to provide additional traction and allow very steep ascents and descents.

Varieties range from lightweight aluminium models intended for walking on snow covered glaciers, to aggressive steel models intended for vertical and overhanging ice and rock. Snowshoes can be used to walk through deep snow.

Glaciers

When travelling over glaciers, crevasses pose a grave danger. These giant cracks in the ice are not always visible as snow can be blown and freeze over the top to make a snow bridge. At times snow bridges can be as thin as a few inches. Climbers use a system of ropes to protect themselves from such hazards.

Basic gear for glacier travel includes crampons[30] and ice axes. Teams of two to five climbers tie into a rope equally spaced. If a climber begins to fall the other members of the team perform a self-arrest[31] to stop the fall. The other members of the team enact a crevasse[32] rescue to pull the fallen climber from the crevasse.

---

29) neve(neivei); 만년설(빙하의 상층부의 입상 빙설)
30) crampons; (등산용) 아이젠
31) self-arrest; (설상 등반 기술) 자기 제동
32) crevasse; 빙하 속의 깊이 갈라진 틈

11. Skiing

Actual Scene

A: Bob, 스키시즌이 왔다, 그렇지 않니?
   The skiing season has come, hasn't it, Bob?

B: 응, 박군, 넌 스키를 좋아하니?
   Yes, are you fond of skiing, Mr. Park?

A: 응, 매우 좋아해, 넌?
   Yes, very. And you?

B: 나도 매우 좋아해. 겨울마다 스키를 가니?
   So am I. Do you go skiing every winter?

A: 응, 적어도 겨울마다 한번은 가지. 3년 전에 스키하는 법을 배웠어. 나는 매년 겨울 무주로 스키하러 가.
   Yes, at least once every winter. I learned how to ski three years ago. I make it a rule to go skiing at Mooju every winter.

B: 오, 너도? 그러면 스키 잘 타겠다, 그렇지 않니?
   Oh, do you? Then you are a good skier, aren't you?

A: 오, 아니, 그렇게 잘 타지 못해. 하지만 스키가 매우 재미있어서 스키에 광적이야. 스키는 겨울 스포츠의 왕이야.
   Oh, no, not so good a skier, but I'm crazy about skiing, because it's so fun. It's the king of winter sports.

B: 응 그래. 스키는 가장 남자다운 스포츠 중 하나라고 믿어. 아무 것도 새 눈으로 쌓인 슬로프를 신속하게 미끄러져 내려오는 것보다 큰 기쁨을 주지는 못해.

III. Sports Activities

So, it is. It's one of the most manly sports, I believe. Nothing gives me a greater pleasure than to glide swiftly down the slope covered with fresh snow.

A: 맞아. 가까운 시일 내에 스키타러 갈래?

Right. Shall we go skiing one of these days?

B: 응, 기꺼이.

Yes, by all means.

III. Sports Activities

Learning Terms

powdery snow
large snow flakes
descent

"There are really only three things to learn in skiing: how to put on your skis, how to slide downhill, and how to walk along the hospital corridor."
- Lord Mancroft

III. Sports Activities

Skiing

Skiing is a group of sports using skis as equipment for traveling over snow. Skis are used in conjunction with[33] boots that connect to the ski with use of a binding.

Skiing can be grouped into two general categories. The older of the two disciplines, originated in Scandinavia and uses free-heel bindings that attach at the toes of the skier's boots but not at the heels.

Types of Nordic skiing include cross-country, ski jumping and Telemark. Alpine skiing (often called 'downhill skiing'), originated in the European Alps, and is characterized by fixed-heel bindings that attach at both the toe and the heel of the skier's boot.

Early history

The Norse goddess Skaði hunts in the mountains on skiis in an illustration (1901) by H. L. M. The earliest people to ski in Fennoscandia may have been the distant ancestors of the modern day Sami.

One of the early names used for the Sami was skridfinner/scricfinni, which some have translated as 'skiing Sami'. Pre-historic Nordic people and Sami used skis to assist in hunting, military maneuvers, and as a practical means of transportation. The oldest and most accurately documented evidence of skiing origins is found in modern day Norway and Sweden.

---

33) in conjunction with ; …와 함께

III. Sports Activities

Types of skiing

Many different types of skiing are popular, especially in colder climates, and many types of competitive skiing events are recognized by the International Olympic Committee(IOC), the International Ski Federation(FIS), and other sporting organizations, such as the U.S. Ski and Snowboard Association in America. Skiing is the most visible to the public during the Winter Olympic Games where it is a major sport.

In skiing's traditional core regions in the snowy parts of Scandinavia, as well as in places such as Alaska, both recreational and competitive skiing is as likely to refer to the cross-country variants[34] as to the internationally downhill variants.

Skiing techniques are difficult to master, and accordingly there are ski schools that teach everything from the basics of turning and stopping safely to more advanced carving, racing, mogul or 'bump' skiing and newer freestyle techniques. There are two primary types of downhill skiing — 'telemark'[35] and 'alpine'[36].

For beginning skiers learning under a trained instructor, skiing speeds are low, the terrain is not steep and is often well-manicured, and the risks are relatively low. For extreme skiers, testing their expert abilities against ever more challenging terrain, the risks may be much higher.

---

34) variants; 변종, 이형(異形)
35) telemark; 스키 점프에서 텔레마크식 회전(한쪽 다리를 앞으로 내밀며 다리를 굽혀 회전·착지하는 기술)
36) alpine; 활강 스키

III. Sports Activities

12. Skating

Actual Scene

A: Bob, 어디 가니?

   Hello, Mr. Bob? Where are you going?

B: 오, 스케이트 타러 가. 2시에 거기서 김 군을 만나기로 했어.

   Oh, I'm going skating. I'm to meet Mr. Kim there at two.

A: 오, 그래. 스케이트 잘 타?

   Oh, are you? Can you skate well?

A: 오, 아니, 잘 못타지만, 스케이트의 기본 원리는 알아. 어린 시절에 스케이트 타는 법을 배웠어. 나와 같이 가는 게 어떠니?

   Oh, no, not so well, but I know the basic principles of skating. I learned how to skate in my childhood. What do you say to coming with me?

B: 고마워. 그런데 스케이트를 잘 못 탈 것 같아.

   Thank you. But I'm afraid I can't skate.

A: 그건 걱정 마. 네가 스케이트 배우기를 원하면, 내가 가르쳐 줄게. 나와 같이 가, 일단 시도를 하면, 분명히 팬이 될 거야.

   Don't worry about that. If you want to learn to skate, I'll teach you myself. Come with me, once you give it a try, you will surely become a fan.

A: 글쎄, 스케이트 타는 법을 가르쳐 줄래?

   Well, you will teach me how to skate?

B: 응, 기꺼이. 그러나 넘어질 각오를 해야 해.

   Yes, with pleasure. But you'd better be prepared for a few falls.

A: 응, 그럴게.
　　Yes, I will.

III. Sports Activities

Learning Terms

ice skate / roller skate / inline skate
figure skating / speed skating
jump / spin / spiral
toe jump / edge jump
single skating / pair skating / ice dancing / synchronized skating
triple axel / spiral sequence / combination spin

"Acting is easier than skating in a way and harder in other aspects. In skating, you get one chance, and with acting you get to do it over and over." - Tara Lipinski

Ice skating

Ice skating is moving on ice by using ice skates. It can be done for a variety of reasons, including leisure, traveling, and various sports. Ice skating occurs both on specially prepared indoor and outdoor tracks, as well as on naturally occurring bodies of frozen water such as lakes and rivers.

History

A study by Federico Formenti of the University of Oxford suggests that the earliest ice skating happened in Southern Finland about 4,000 years ago.

Originally, skates were merely sharpened, flattened bone strapped to the bottom of the foot. Skaters did not actually skate on the ice, but rather glided on top of it.

True skating emerged when a steel blade with sharpened edges was used. Skates now cut into the ice instead of gliding on top of it. Adding edges to ice skates was invented by the Dutch in the 13th or 14th century. These ice skates were made of steel, with sharpened edges on the bottom to aid movement. The construction of modern ice skates has stayed largely the same.

Physical mechanics of skating

Ice skating works because the metal blade at the bottom of the skate shoe can glide with very little friction over the surface of the ice.

However, slightly leaning the blade over and digging one of its edges into the ice('rock over and bite') gives skaters the ability to increase friction and control their movement at will.

They can also create momentum by pushing the blade against the curved track which cuts into the ice. Skillfully combining these two actions of leaning and pushing - a technique known as 'drawing' - results in what looks like effortless and graceful curvilinear[37] flow across the ice. How the low-friction surface develops is not known exactly, but a large body of knowledge does exist.

Dangers

The primary danger in ice skating is falling on the ice. The chance of falling depends on the roughness of the ice, the design of the ice skate, and the skill and experience of the skater. While serious injury is rare, a number of(short track) skaters have been paralysed after a fall when they hit the boarding. An additional danger of falling is injury caused by the skater's own metal blades or those of other skaters.

The second, and more serious, danger is falling through the ice into the freezing water underneath when skating outdoors on a frozen body of water. This can lead to serious injury or death due to shock, hypothermia[38] or drowning.

---

37) curvilinear; 곡선으로 이루어진
38) hypothermia; 저체온증

13. Golf

Actual Scene

A: 만나서 반가워. 잘 지내니?

   Nice to meet you. How are you?

B: 나도 만나서 반가워.

   Nice to meet you, too.

A: 우리는 다음 8시간 동안 골프의 기본 테크닉을 배울 거야. 전에 골프를 했니?

   We will learn about the basic techniques of golf during the next 8 classes. Have you played golf before?

B: 아니, 한 적이 없어. 그러나 재미있고 사교적인 스포츠라고 생각해.

   No, I haven't. But I think it is an interesting and sociable sport.

A: 그래. 일반적으로, 많은 사람들은 골프가 사치스러운 스포츠라고 생각해. 그들 중 많은 사람들이 장래에 골프를 함께 즐길 거야.

   Surely. Generally, lots of people think that golf is a luxurious sport. Many of them will enjoy it together in the future.

B: 골프는 점점 너 대중화될 거야. 나도 골프하는 것을 배우고 싶지만, 너무 어려울 것 같아.

   Golf is said to become more and more popular. I'd like to learn to play it, but I wonder if it is too difficult for me.

A: 너에게 달렸어. 골프는 주의 깊은 연습이 필요해. 그것은 플레이어가 코스를 따라 볼을 홀에 쳐 넣는 게임이야. 일반적으로 프로 골프는 18홀 매치야. 코

III. Sports Activities

스를 마치는 데 최저타를 한 플레이어가 게임을 이기는 거야.

It depends on you. Golf requires careful practice. It is a game in which a player hits a ball into a hole along a course. There are generally 18-hole matches in professional golf. The player who use fewest strokes to complete the course wins the game.

III. Sports Activities

Learning Terms

caddie
drive / wood / iron / putter
fairway / green / hazard / rough
hole in one / eagle / birdie / par / bogey
slice / hook
stance / address / swing / impact / follow throw / finish

"If I had to choose between my wife and my putter, well, I'd miss her."
- Gray Player(golf player)

Golf

Golf is a precision club-and-ball sport, in which competing players(golfers), using many types of clubs, attempt to hit balls into each hole on a golf course while employing the fewest number of strokes. Golf is one of the few ball games that does not require a standardized playing area.

Instead, the game is played on golf 'courses', each of which features a unique design, although courses typically consist of either 9 or 18 holes. Golf is defined, in the rules of golf, as 'playing a ball with a club from the teeing ground into the hole by a stroke or successive strokes in accordance with the Rules'.

Golf competition is generally played for the lowest number of strokes by an individual, known simply as stroke play, or the lowest score on the most individual holes during a complete round by an individual or team, known as match play.

Origin

The origin of golf is unclear and open to debate. Some historians trace the sport back to the Roman game of paganica, in which participants used a bent stick to hit a stuffed leather ball.

One theory asserts that paganica spread throughout Europe as the Romans conquered most of the continent, during the first century B.C., and eventually evolved into the modern game.

Others cite Chuiwan('chui' means striking and 'wan' means small ball) as the progenitor[39], a Chinese game played between the eighth and 14th centuries. A Ming Dynasty scroll dating back to 1368 entitled 'The Autumn Banquet', shows a member of the Chinese Imperial court swinging what appears to be a golf club at a small ball with the aim of sinking it into a hole.

Play of the game

Every round of golf is based on playing a number of holes in a given order. A round typically consists of 18 holes that are played in the order determined by the course layout. On a nine-hole course, a standard round consists of two consecutive nine-hole rounds.

Playing a hole on a golf course is initiated by putting a ball into play by striking it with a club on the teeing area(also called the 'tee box' or simply 'the tee'.)

When the initial shot on a hole is a long-distance shot intended to move the ball a great distance down the fairway, this shot is commonly called a 'drive'. Shorter holes generally are initiated with 'shorter' clubs. Once the ball comes to rest, the golfer strikes it again as many times as necessary using shots that are variously known as a lay-up, an approach, a 'pitch', or a chip, until the ball reaches the green, where he or she then putts the ball into the hole(commonly called 'sinking the putt').

---

39) progenitor; (사람·동식물의) 조상, 창시자, 선임자

III. Sports Activities

14. The Olympics

Actual Scene

A: 나는 올림픽 경기에 대해 아무것도 몰라. 올림픽 경기가 무엇인지 설명해 줄 수 있니?

I don't know anything about the Olympic Games. Could you explain what they are?

B: 어, 글쎄. 국제적인 스포츠 축제라고 불리지.

Well, let me see. They might be called an international sports festival.

A: 올림픽 경기의 아이디어를 누가 먼저 생각했지?

Who ever thought of the idea of the Olympic Games first?

B: 고대 그리스 사람들이 했어. 그들은 매 4년마다 올림픽 경기를 개최했어.

The ancient Greeks did. They held those games every four years.

A: 최초의 경기가 열린 것이 얼마 전이었나?

How long ago was it that the first games were held?

B: 기원전 776년에 최초의 경기가 열렸다고 해.

It is said that the first ones were held in 776 B.C.

A: 그때 이후로 올림픽이 계속 열려왔나요?

Have they been held ever since that time?

B: 아니, 394년에 중단됐어. 1896년에 아테네에서 근대올림픽이 처음으로 부활됐어.

No, they stopped in A.D. 394. In 1896, the modern Olympic Games were first revived at Athens.

III. Sports Activities

A: '올림픽'이라는 이름이 어디서 유래되었는지 궁금해.

　　I wonder where the name 'Olympic' comes from.

B: 그것은 그리스 선수들이 경기를 위해 모인 그리스에 있는 산을 따라 이름 지어졌어.

　　It is named after a mountain in Greece, where the Greek athletes gathered for the games.

A: 마지막 올림픽이 열린 곳을 기억하니?

　　Do you remember where the last Olympic Games were held?

B: 응, 기억해. 런던에서 2012년에.

　　Yes, I do. In London in 2012.

III. Sports Activities

Learning Terms

athlete
field
marathon race
weight-lifting / judo / wrestling / boxing
sacred fire
gold medal / silver medal / bronze medal

"The six colours, including the white background, represent the colours of all the world's flags- this is a true international emblem."
- Pierre de Coubertin

The Olympic games

The Olympic games

The Olympic Games are competitions between athletes in individual or team events and not between countries. They bring together the athletes designated for such purpose by their respective NOCs, whose entries have been accepted by the IOC, and who compete under the technical direction of the IFs [International (Sports) Federation] concerned.

The authority of last resort on any question concerning the Olympic Games rests in IOC. The Olympic Games consist of the Games of the Olympiad and the Olympic Winter Games. Both take place every four years.

The first Olympic Winter Games were celebrated in 1924. Starting from that date, they are numbered in the order in which they are held, the XVII Olympic Winter Games being however held in 1994. Only those sports which are practised on snow and ice are considered as winter sports.

The duration of the Games of the Olympiad and of Olympic Winter Games shall not exceed sixteen days, including the day of the opening ceremony. If no competition is scheduled for Sundays or public holidays, the duration of the Olympic Games may, with the approval of the IOC Executive Board, be extended accordingly.

The Olympiad

The term 'Olympiad' designates the period of four successive years

III. Sports Activities

which begins with the Games of the Olympiad and ends with the opening of the Games of the following Olympiad.

If, for any reason, the Games of any Olympiad are not celebrated, the Olympiad expires four years from the day of its beginning, upon which date a new Olympiad begins.

The Olympiads are numbered consecutively from the first Olympic Games(Games of the Olympiad) of modern times, celebrated in Athens in 1896.

The Olympic symbol

The five colours of the rings are mandatorily blue, yellow, black, green and red. The rings are interlaced from left to right. The blue, black and red rings are situated at the top, the yellow and green rings at the bottom.

The whole approximately forms a regular trapezium[40] , of which the small base is the inferior, according to the official design deposited at the IOC headquarters.

The Olympic symbol represents the union of the five continents and the meeting of the athletes from throughout the world at the Olympic Games.

Opening and Closing Ceremonies

The Olympic Games shall be proclaimed open by the Head of State of the host country.

The Head of State is received at the entrance of the stadium by the

---

40) trapezium; [trəpiːziəm]사다리꼴

President of the IOC and by the President of the OCOG[41]. The two Presidents then show the Head of State into his box in the official stand.

The parade of the participants then follows. Each delegation, dressed in its official uniform, must be preceded by a name-board bearing its names and must be accompanied by its flag to be carried by a member of the delegation.

The flags of the participating delegations, as well as the name-boards, shall be provided by the OCOG and shall all be of equal size. The name-board-bearers shall be designated by the OCOG.

No participant in the parade is permitted to carry flags, banners, banderoles[42], cameras or other visible accessories or objects which are not part of his uniform.

The delegations parade in alphabetical order according to the language of the host country, except for Greece, which leads the parade, and for the host country, which brings up the rear. Only those athletes participating in the Olympic Games with the right to accommodation in the Olympic Village may take part in the parade, led by a maximum of six officials per delegation.

The delegations salute the Head of State and President of the IOC as they as they walk past their box. Each delegation, after completing its march, proceeds to the seats which have been reserved for it in order to watch the ceremony, with the exception of its flag bearer who remains on the field.

---

41) OCOG: Organizing Committees for the Olympic Games
42) banderol(e): (창, 돛대에 다는) 작은 기

III. Sports Activities

The President of the IOC, accompanied by the President of the OCOG, proceeds to the rostrum[43] positioned on the field in front of the official stand. The President of the OCOG gives an address lasting a maximum of three minutes, then adds these words, "I have the honour of inviting....., President of the International Olympic Committee, to speak".

The President of the IOC then gives a speech, adding: "I have the honour of inviting....., (the head of State) to proclaim open the Games of the .....th Olympiad of the modern era(or the....th Olympic Winter Games)."

The Head of State proclaims the Games open by saying: "I declare open the Games of ...(names of City) celebrating the...th Olympiad of the modern era (or the ...th Olympic Winter Games)."

While the Olympic hymn is being played, the Olympic flag unfurled horizontally is brought into the stadium and hoisted on the flagpole erected in the arena.

The Olympic torch is brought into the stadium by runners relaying each other. The last runner circles the track before lighting the Olympic flame, which shall not be extinguished until the closing of the Olympic Games. The lighting of the Olympic flame shall be followed by symbolic release of pigeons.

The flag bearers of all the delegations form a semi-circle around the rostrum. A competitor of the host country mounts the rostrum. Holding a corner of the Olympic flag in his left hand, and raising his

---

43) rostrum: 연단

right hand, he takes the following solemn oath: "In the name of all the competitors I promise that we take part in these Olympic Games, respecting and abiding by the rules which govern them, in the true spirit of sportsmanship, for the glory of sport and the honour of our teams."

Immediately afterwards, a judge form the host country mounts the rostrum and, in the same manner, takes the following oath:" In the name of all the judges and officials, I promise that we shall officiate in these Olympic Games with complete impartiality, respecting and abiding by the rules which govern them, in the true spirit of sportsmanship."

IV. Attendance in the Olympics

1. Briefing and Business
2. Access Control
3. Check-in and Check-out
4. At a Lodging Area
5. At the Information Center
6. International Cooperation
7. The Flag Raising Ceremony
8. Meal Service
9. The Amenities
10. Games Management
11. At the International Airport
12. On the Playing Field
13. In a Team Bus
14. At the Ticket Office
15. In the Hotel Lobby

IV. Attendance in the Olympics

1. Briefing and Business
(브리핑과 업무)

1) Olympic Village Parking Lot (올림픽 선수촌 주차장)

1-1　올림픽 선수촌에 오신 걸 환영합니다.
　　　Welcome to the Olympic Village!

1-2　(저는) 당신을 VIP응접실로 모시겠습니다.
　　　I will escort you to the VIP reception room.

1-3　이곳은 선수와 임원을 위한 등록이나 다른 행정업무를 처리하는 사무실입니다.
　　　This is the office that handles the accreditation and other administrative affairs for athletes and officials.

2) Reception room (응접실)

2-1　당신의 이름을 방문자 기록부(방명록)에 기입해 주시겠어요?
　　　Would you please fill your name in the visitors' register?

2-2　올림픽 선수촌장께서 당신에게 조그마한 선물을 증정할 것입니다.
　　　The Mayor of Olympic Village will present a small gift to you.

2-3　상황실로 옮겨 올림픽 선수촌이 어떻게 기능을 하는지(운영되는지) 보실까요?
　　　May we move on to the Report Room to see how the Olympic Village functions?

IV. Attendance in the Olympics

3) Report Room (상황실)

3-1   이곳은 올림픽 선수촌의 다양한 직무(역할)를 위한 중추부서입니다.
This is the Central Post for the various functions of the Olympic Village.

3-2   Mr. Kim, 우리의 운영직원이 올림픽 선수촌의 행정에 대해 간단한 브리핑을 해드릴 겁니다.
Mr. Kim, our operational staff will give you a short briefing on the administration of the Olympic Village.

3-3   편하게 질문하십시오.
Please feel free to ask questions.

3-4   그러면 선수홀 근처의 올림픽 서비스센터로 나아갑시다.
Let us then proceed to the Olympic Service Center near the Athletes' Hall.

4) Olympic Service Center (올림픽 서비스 센터)

4-1   이곳은 올림픽 서비스 센터입니다.
This is Olympic service center.

4-2   이 센터는 전신, 인쇄, 일반적인 운영 지원과 올림픽 회의 준비와 같은 서비스를 제공합니다.
This center offers such services as telex, printing, general operational support and Olympic conference preparations.

4-3   이 센터는 아침 8시부터 저녁9시까지 엽니다.
This center opens from 8 a.m. till 9 p.m.

4-4   우리는 지금 스포츠 안내센터로 이동할 것입니다.
We will now move to the Sports Information Center.

Ⅳ. Attendance in the Olympics

4-5   우리가 가는 길에 은행, 종합 안내 센터와 비디오룸을 지나갈 것입니다.
We will pass through a bank, the General Information Center and a video room on our way.

5) Sports Information Center (스포츠 안내 센터)

5-1   이 센터는 경기일정, 결과 그리고 경기장/훈련 장소에 대한 정보를 제공합니다.
This center supplies information on games schedules, results, and the competition venue/training sites.

5-2   이 센터는 아침 8시부터 저녁 9시까지 운영합니다.
This center runs from 8 a.m. till 9 p.m.

5-3   우리는 지금 관광과 관련된 포스터가 전시된 홀로 갈 것입니다.
We will now go to the hall where the posters related to sightseeing are exhibited.

6. Exhibition Hall (전시관)

6-1   이 홀은 모든 관광정보를 얻기 좋은 장소입니다. 왜냐하면 여기에 한국의 모든 관광지가 소개되기 때문입니다.
This hall is a good place to get all the sightseeing information, because all the tourist resorts of Korea are introduced here.

6-2   이 홀은 아침 8시부터 저녁 9시까지 엽니다.
This hall opens from 9:00 in the morning till 9:00 at night.

6-3   그러면 쇼핑센터로 갑시다.
Let's go to the shopping center, then.

Ⅳ. Attendance in the Olympics

7) Shopping Center (쇼핑센터)

7-1   쇼핑센터는 올림픽 선수촌 거주자의 편의를 위해 기념품, 전통공예품, 생활필수품 그리고 스포츠용품과 같은 다양한 물품을 갖추고 있습니다.
The shopping center furnishes various goods such as souvenirs, traditional art crafts, daily necessities. and sporting goods for the convenience of Olympic Village residents.

7-2   쇼핑센터는 오전 9시부터 오후 9시까지 엽니다.
The shopping center also opens from 9 a.m. to 9 p.m.

7-3   지금 디스코텍으로 갈까요?
Shall we go to the discotheque now?

8) Discotheque (디스코텍)

8-1   이 디스코텍은 선수와 임원을 위한 레크리에이션 센터입니다. 그리고 술은 금지되지만 음료를 무료로 제공합니다.
This discotheque is the recreation center for athletes and officials, and offers soft drinks free of charge, though hard liquor is prohibited.

8-2   이 장소는 아침 8시에서 자정까지 엽니다.
This place is open between 8 a.m. and midnight.

8-3   이제 극장으로 이동합시다.
Let us move to the theater now.

9) Movie Theater (극장)

9-1   한국영화와 일반 홍보영상이 여기서 상영됩니다. 또한 다양한 공연뿐만 아니라 전통무용과 현대무용이 공연될 것입니다.

Korean movies and general films for publicity are shown here. Also traditional dances and modern dances as well as a variety of public performances will be staged here.

9-2 극장은 500명의 수용 좌석을 가지고 있습니다.
The theater has a seating capacity of 500 people.

9-3 영화는 하루 2번 오후 3시와 10시에 9월 3일부터 10월 2일까지 올림픽기간 동안 상영될 것입니다.
Movies will be shown twice a day between 3p.m. and 10 p.m. starting from September 3, to October 2 during the Olympiad.

9-4 9월 17일부터 10월 1일까지 많은 다양한 공연이 있을 것입니다.
There will be many different performances from September 17 to October 1.

9-5 저희는 다음에 국기게양식을 포함한 몇 가지 축제가 열릴 국기광장을 방문하겠습니다.
We will next visit the flag plaza where several festivals including the flag-raising ceremony are to take place.

10) Flag Plaza (국기 광장)

10-1 206개 IOC회원국의 국기(깃발)가 올림픽 경기 전(全) 기간 동안 휘날리게 될 것입니다.
The flags of 206 IOC member countries will be flying during the entire period of the Olympic Games.

10-2 9월 16일 선수촌 축제를 시작으로 10월 1일 고별의 밤까지 매머드 쇼가 매일 이 광장에서 열릴 것입니다.
There will be mammoth shows in this plaza everyday beginning with the Village festival on September 16 to the farewell night on

IV. Attendance in the Olympics

October 1.

10-3 지금 식당으로 갑시다.
Let's go to the dining hall now.

11) Dining Hall (식당)

11-1 이 식당은 동시에 1,500명까지 모실(서브할) 수 있습니다.
This dining hall can serve 1,500 people at the same time.

11-2 음식은 하루에 3번 제공될 것입니다.
Meals will be supplied three times a day.

11-3 이곳은 셀프서비스를 기본으로 한 식당입니다.
This is a cafeteria on a self-service basis.

11-4 메뉴는 음식전문가에 의해 종교적, 지역적 특성에 따라 배열됩니다.
The menu is arranged according to religious and regional characteristics by food experts.

11-5 같은 메뉴가 5일마다 반복됩니다.
The same menu will be repeated every 5 days.

11-6 가능한 한 많은 서빙을 할 수(먹고 싶은만큼 먹을 수)있습니다.
You may have as many servings as possible.

11-7 레스토랑은 아침 5시부터 오후 11시까지 엽니다.
The restaurant is open from 5 a.m. to 11 p.m.

11-8 다음은 선수와 임원 숙소로 가겠습니다.
We will next go to the lodging area for athletes and officials.

12) Lodging Area (숙소)

12-1 9층에서 18층 사이의 18개 아파트(건물) 동이 있습니다.
There are 18 apartment buildings of 9 to 18 floors.

12-2 총 1,356개의 아파트 호실이 있습니다. 각 방의 크기는 113평방제곱미터에서 211평방제곱미터까지 다양합니다.
There are a total of 1,356 apartment units. The size of each room varies from 113 square meters to 211 square meters.

12-3 한 개의 호실은 4명에서 9명의 선수나 임원이 함께 씁니다.(한 개의 호실을 선수 또는 임원 4~9명이 함께 쓴다.)
One apartment unit will be shared by 4 to 9 athletes or officials.

12-4 아파트는 비슷한 언어, 관습 또는 종교적인 배경의 국민들이 서로 인접해 머물도록 배정됩니다.
The apartments are assigned in order that the nationals of a similar language, custom or religious background may stay adjacent to each other.

12-5 선수촌 관리사무실과 라운지는 1층에 있으며, 대표단 사무실은 2층에 있습니다.
The Village Management office and the Lounge are located on the first floor, and the Delegation offices on the second floor.

13) International Area (국제관)

13-1 선수의 홀은 오락시설과 쇼핑센터를 그 안에 갖추고 있습니다.
The Athletes' Hall has entertainment facilities and a shopping center in it.

13-2 선수의 홀은 지상 3층과 지하실이 있습니다.
The Athletes' Hall has 3 stories above and abasement.

Ⅳ. Attendance in the Olympics

13-3 지하실에는 디스코텍이 있습니다.

There is a discotheque in the basement.

13-4 1층에 우체국, 통신 서비스 사무실, 은행 지점, 서비스 센터, 안내센터, 전시홀이 있습니다.

On the first floor, you will find a post office, a telecommunication service office, a bank branch, a service center, an information center, and an exhibition hall.

13-5 1층에, 또 다른 전시관, 비디오 게임장, 탁구장, 그리고 극장이 있습니다.

On the first floor, there are another exhibition hall, a video game room, a table tennis room, and a theater.

13-6 수영장, 샤워장, 그리고 계체실(체중측정실)이 선수홀 별관에 있습니다.

A swimming pool, shower rooms, and the weigh-in room are located in the annex to the Athletes' Hall.

14) Epilogue (끝맺음)

14-1 저희는 지금 올림픽선수촌 순회(라운드)를 마쳤습니다.

We have now completed the round of the Olympic Village.

14-2 올림픽선수촌에서 일하는 저희 모두는 참가자들이 최상의 컨디션으로 경기에 참가하고, 우정과 국제 친선의 정을 나누도록 편안하고 쾌적한 환경을 만들기 위해 최선을 다합니다.

All of us working in the Olympic Village are doing our best for their pleasant and comfortable stay so that they may play the games in their best condition, and share friendship and international good will.

14-3 감사합니다. 안녕히 가십시오.

Thank you very much. Good-bye.

IV. Attendance in the Olympics

2. Access Control
(출입통제)

1-1 외 1문 출입안내소에서 임시출입증을 요구하세요.
Please ask for a temporary pass at the Access Information booth at the Outer gate No. 1.

1-2 따라오세요. 제가 도와 드리겠습니다.
Please follow me. I will help you.

1-3 제가 무엇을 도와 드릴까요?
What can I do for you?

1-4 사전에 올림픽선수촌 방문허가를 받았나요?
Have you obtained a permit to visit the Olympic Village in advance?

1-5 당신의 AD카드를 볼 수 있나요?
May I see your AD card?

1-6 잠시만 기다려주세요. 제가 관련 부서에 연락해볼게요.
Please wait a moment. I will contact the office concerned.

1-7 미안하지만 당신은 사전에(미리) 출입허가를 받지 않았기 때문에 들어갈 수가 없습니다. 다음에 다시 해주시겠어요?
I am sorry, but you are not allowed to enter since you have not obtained a permit beforehand. Will you please try next time?

1-8 올림픽선수촌 어디를 방문하고 싶으십니까?
Which part of the Olympic Village do you want to visit?

1-9 미안하지만 올림픽선수촌 숙박시설의 출입은 제한되어 있습니다.

Ⅳ. Attendance in the Olympics

I am sorry, but the access to the lodging area of the Olympic Village is restricted.

1-10 당신이 방문하고자 하는 곳이 어디에 있는지 아십니까?
Do you know where the place you want to visit is located?

1-11 길 건너편에 있는 방문자주차장에 주차해야 합니다.
You may park your car in the visitors' parking lot across the road.

1-12 올림픽 선수촌을 떠날 때는 반드시 이 사무실에 임시출입증을 반납하고 신분증을 찾아가세요.
When you leave the Olympic Village, please be sure to return the temporary pass to this office and get your ID card back.

1-13 당신이 떠날 때 ID카드를 저기 check-out post에 맡겨놓을 테니 차량출입증과 임시출입증을 거기에 반납하고 당신의 ID카드를 받아가세요.
I will turn your ID card over to the check-out post over there when you leave. You must also return your vehicle pass and temporary pass there and get your ID card back.

1-14 이 주차장은 VIP출입증을 가지고 있는 차량 예약용입니다. 당신은 우회전해서 방문객주차장에 주차해 주시겠습니까?
This parking lot is reserved for vehicles with VIP passes. Will you please turn right, and park your car in the visitors' parking lot?

1-15 미안하지만 리포터들은 내문 3번과 4번을 사용하게 되어 있습니다.
I am sorry, but reporters are supposed to use Inner gate No. 3 and No. 4.

1-16 올림픽선수촌의 숙소에 방문하고자 하는 사람들은 행정센터에 있는 출입통제사무실에 문의하시길 바랍니다.
Those who wish to visit the lodging area of the Olympic Village are asked to inquire at the Access Control Office at the Administration Center.

Ⅳ. Attendance in the Olympics

1-17 이 문은 선수나, 팀 임원, 운영요원만 이용할 수 있습니다. 당신은 이 보도를 따라 외 1문 출입안내소에 문의 하시는 게 좋습니다. 이 출입구는 기자들이 출입하는 곳이 아닙니다. 올림픽 선수촌 외 1문을 사용하세요.
This gate is only for athletes, team officials, and operation members. You'd better follow this sidewalk, and inquire at the Access Information Booth at the Outer gate No. 1. This gate is not for the press. Please use the Olympic Village gate No. 1.

1-18 이 문은 차량이 통행하는 곳이 아닙니다. 돌아가셔서 외 1문으로 가세요.
This gate is not for vehicles. Please turn back, and go to the Outer gate No. 1.

1-19 차량들은 통행증이 없으면 올림픽선수촌에 허락되지 않습니다. 당신은 주차장에 차를 주차하시고 걸어 들어가세요.
Vehicles are not allowed in the Olympic Village without a pass. You may park your car in the parking lot, and walk in.

1-20 리포터들은 올림픽선수촌 관리자에 의해 발급된 허가증 없이는 올림픽 선수촌 건물에 들어갈 수가 없습니다.
Reporters are not allowed in the buildings of the Olympic Village without a permit issued by Olympic Village administrator.

1-21 AD카드 또는 임시출입증에 'R'이 코딩된 사람들만이 숙박지역에 들어갈 수 있습니다. 만일 당신이 그곳에 방문을 계획하신다면 행정센터에 있는 출입봉제소에 문의하시기 바랍니다.
Only those whose AD cards or temporary passes are coded by 'R' are allowed in the lodging area. If you plan to visit there, please inquire at the Access Control in the Administration Center.

Ⅳ. Attendance in the Olympics

3. Check-in and Check-out
(입실과 퇴실)

1) Check-in/out and Accommodation Fee (입실/퇴실과 숙박료)

1-1 안녕하세요. 저희는 여기에서 각 대표단의 입실과 퇴실 및 숙박비를 담당하고 있습니다.

Hello, here we are in charge of the check-in and check-out and Accommodation Fees of each delegation.

1-2 제가 담당매니저입니다. 저희는 대표단의 이동을 올림픽선수촌의 도착에서 퇴실까지 계속해서 파악(추적)합니다.

I am the manager in charge. We keep track of the movements of delegations from their arrival to the final check-out from the Olympic Village.

1-3 각 나라는 도착하기 전 미리 각국 참가자들을 위해 일정수의 방을 배정받을 것입니다. 배정서는 도착함과 동시에 프런트 데스크에 제출되어야 합니다. 각 국은 특정 개인들을 다양한 종류의 방, 즉 호실에 배정하는 책임이 있습니다.

Each country will be previously been assigned a certain number of rooms for its participants before arriving. This assignment sheet must be presented upon arrival at the front desk. Each country has the responsibility of assigning specific individuals to various rooms, or units.

1-4 대표단의 이동과 관련하여 가장 큰 문제는 사람의 수와 신원의 불확실성입니다. 사절단장은 숙박료가 정확하게 계산되어 지불되기 위해 숙박하

IV. Attendance in the Olympics

는(거주하는) 사람의 수를 정확히 해주시길 정중히 요구합니다.

The biggest problem with the movements of delegations is the uncertainty of the number of persons and their identification. The Chef de Mission is cordially requested to inform the exact number of persons in residence so that the accommodation fee may be correctly computed and paid.

1-5 지금, 숙박료 담당자가 당신을 안내해드릴 겁니다.

Now, the manager in charge of Accommodation Fees will guide you.

1-6 여기 숙박을 위해 당신의 대표단이 미리 선불한 미화 20만 달러에 대한 영수증이 있습니다. 이제, 미화 6,720달러의 IOC보조금을 추가하여 숙박비는 총 미화 106,720달러입니다.

Here is the receipt for your delegation's advance deposit of US $200,000 for accommodation. Now we add the IOC assistance of US $6,720 and your accommodation fee totals US $106,720.

1-7 대표단의 숙박료가 실제 거주하는 사람의 수에 따라 매일 청구(송장)되어집니다. 계산서는 매 3일마다 당신에게 전달될 것입니다.

The Accommodation Fee of your delegation will be invoiced every day according to the actual number of persons in residence, and a bill will be forwarded to you every three days.

1-8 숙박료는 퇴실하기 2일전까지 완불되어야합니다. 지출이 보증금(선금)을 초과할 경우, 당신은 잔금을 더 지불해야합니다. 하지만 그보다 적을 경우 환불받을 것입니다.

The accommodation fee must be paid up by 2 days before check-out. In case the expenditure exceeds the deposit, you will pay the remainder, but you will get a refund in case the expenditure is less than the deposit.

1-9 대표단의 일부가 보조선수촌이나 부산 요트선수촌에 잠시 머물 경우에도

Ⅳ. Attendance in the Olympics

숙박료는 서울에 있는 올림픽선수촌에만 지불해야합니다.

Even if part of your delegation happens to stay at a Sub Village or at the Busan Yachting Village, the Accommodation Fee will be paid only at the Olympic Village in Seoul.

1-10 안내를 드리면, 청구서의 발행(발급) 같은 요금과 관련된 서류업무는 여기에서 처리하지만 실제 지불 또는 환불은 은행에서 처리합니다.

For your information, I must tell you that the paperwork relating to the fee such as the issuance of invoices will be handled here, but actual payment or refunding will be handled at the bank.

1-11 관련 대표단이 올림픽 선수촌에서 퇴실하고 AD넘버가 MSR로부터 지워지면 일일 요금청구는 끝납니다.

The daily invoicing will be terminated when the delegation concerned checks out of the Olympic Village and the AD number is thus erased from MSR(Magnetic Stripe Reader).

1-12 올림픽 선수촌에 거주할 대표단의 인원수가 확인되었고 그와 관련된 문제가 처리되었기 때문에, AD카드 발급을 위해 등록 센터로 가세요.

Now that the number of delegation members to reside at the Olympic Village has been ascertained, and the related matters have been taken care of, you may proceed to the Accreditation Center for AD cards.

2) Issuance of Accreditation Card (AD카드 발급)

2-1 당신의 국적과 이름을 말씀해 주시겠어요?

Could you tell me your nationality and name?

2-2 여기에 사인해 주세요.

Please sign here.

2-3 사진을 찍기 위해 저기로 이동해 주세요.

Please move over there for a photograph.

2-4 당신의 카드가 만들어지는 동안 잠깐만 기다리세요.
Please wait a moment while your card is made up.

2-5 여기 카드가 있습니다. 우리는 지금 숙소로 갈 것입니다.
Here is your card. We will now go to the lodging area.

3) Assignment of Lodging (숙소배정)

3-1 당신의 대표단은 아파트 101동, 202호실을 사용할 것입니다.
Your delegation will occupy apartment building 101, lodging unit, 202.

3-2 대표단장이 숙박 배정서를 작성해서 통역원에게 가능한 한 빨리 가져다주길 바랍니다. 그 통역원은 그것을 하우징 서비스 사무실에 가져다줄 것입니다.
We would like to ask the Chief de Mission to fill out a lodging assignment sheet and give it to your interpreter as soon as possible, who will take it to the Housing Service Office.

3-3 당신의 대표단 사무실은 2층에 있습니다.
Your delegation office is located on the 2nd floor.

3-4 당신의 대표단사무실에 있는 장비와 물품을 배정서와 대조해서 확인해 주시고 모든 것이 정확하다면 영수증에 사인해 주세요.
Please check the equipment and supplies at your delegation office against the disposition statement, and sign the receipt if all is correct.

3-5 당신은 이 순간부터 당신이 올림픽촌을 퇴실할 때까지 대표단 사무실을 책임집니다.
You are in charge of your delegation office from this moment until your check-out from the Olympic Village.

3-6 당신의 대표단은 사무실의 장비와 물품의 어떠한 파손과 분실에 대한 책

IV. Attendance in the Olympics

임을 지게 될 것입니다.

Your delegation will be responsible for any damage or loss to the equipment and supplies in the office.

3-7 물품과 장비의 반환에 대한 서류에 사인해 주세요.

Please sign the form for the returning of supplies and equipment.

4. At a Lodging Area
(숙소에서)

1. 방을 청소해 드릴까요?
   May I clean the room?

2. 나중에 청소해 드릴게요.
   I will clean it later.

3. 통역안내원한테 물어 보세요.
   Please ask the guide-interpreter.

4. 미안하지만, 당신이 숙소에 들어갈 수 가 없습니다.
   I am sorry, but you are not allowed to enter the lodging area.

5. 한국 대표단 사무실은 201호실에 있습니다.
   The KOR delegation office is located at room 201.

6. 잠시만 기다려 주세요.
   Please wait a moment.

7. 사용 지침서는 각각의 장비 맨 위쪽 끝에 부착되어 있습니다.
   The instructions for use are attached to the upper end of each equipment.

8. 다리미, 세탁기, 드라이기는 셀프서비스로 이용할 수 있습니다.
   Irons, washing machines, and driers are available for self-service.

9. 12시간 이내에 방 배정을 보고해주세요.
   Please give me a report on room assignments within 12 hours.

10. 우리는 방 배정을 각 NOC 대표단장에게 위임합니다.
    We entrust the assignment of rooms to the Head of each NOC delegation.

IV. Attendance in the Olympics

11. 숙박 배정은 각 NOC단위로 성별 구분 없이 전체적으로 되었습니다.

    Lodging arrangements have been made to accommodate each NOC as a whole without gender based discrimination.

12. 각 아파트 동의 출입구 프런트데스크에 키를 두고 떠나세요.

    Please leave your key at the front desk of each apartment building entrance.

13. 우리는 당신이 체크인에 싸인 한 용지와 대조해서 장비, 가구, 고정시설물의 상태를 점검할 것입니다. 만일 체크아웃 때 그들 중의 일부가 파손이나 분실되면 당신에게 보상을 요구할 것입니다.

    We will check the condition of equipment, furniture, and fixtures against the sheet you had signed upon your check-in. If any of them is found damaged or lost upon your check-out, you will be required to make compensation.

14. 우리가 장비, 가구, 고정시설물뿐만 아니라 숙소상태를 점검할 수 있도록 적어도 체크아웃 72시간 전에 우리에게 알려주시기 바랍니다.

    You are requested to inform us at least 72 hours before your check-out so that we can check the condition of your lodging as well as equipment, furniture, and fixtures.

15. 당신의 방에서 파손이나 분실은 우리에게 책임이 없습니다. 그러므로 확실히 각 방의 벽장을 사용하거나 대표단의 금고를 사용하셔야 됩니다. 당신이 떠날 때는 숙소의 현관문은 물론 그것들을 잠그시기 바랍니다.

    We are not responsible for any damage or loss in your room. Therefore, please be sure to make use of the closets in each unit or the safe in the delegation office. You are advised to lock them as well as the front door of the lodging unit when you go out.

IV. Attendance in the Olympics

5. At the Information Center
(안내센터에서)

A: 안녕하세요!

   Good morning!

B: 무엇을 도와드릴까요?

   What can I do for you?

A: 저는 체조경기장으로 향하는 셔틀버스 시간표를 알고 싶어요.

   I'd like to know the shuttle bus schedule for gymnastics hall.

B: 체조경기장으로 향하는 셔틀버스는 정문 3번 주차장에서 오전 10시에 출발합니다.

   The shuttle bus for gymnastics hall leaves the parking lot No. 3 at the main gate at 10 a.m.

A: 부산 보조선수촌으로 갈 수 있는 교통수단을 알려주세요.

   Please let me know the means of transportation that can take me to Busan Sub Village.

B: 당신이 부산 보조선수촌으로 가기 위해 대중 교통수단을 이용해야 할 것 같습니다. 비행기, 고속버스, 그리고 기차를 이용할 수 있습니다.

   I am afraid you will have to use public transportation to go to Busan Sub Village. Planes, express buses, and trains are available.

A: 저는 명동 근처의 롯데 쇼핑센터로 가길 원합니다. 당신은 친절하게 택시나 렌트카를 불러줄 수 있나요? 또 연습 장소를 어디에서 요청할 수 있나요?

   I want to go to the Lotte Shopping Center near Myeong-dong. Will you kindly call a taxi or a rent-car for me? Also where can I request a place

IV. Attendance in the Olympics

　　 for the practice site?

B: 종합 안내센터 근방의 스포츠안내센터로 가서, 스포츠담당 매니저에게 요청하세요.

　 Please go to the Sports Information Center adjacent to the General Information Center, and ask the manager in charge of the sport.

A: 저는 오늘 선수촌 극장의 영화 시간표와 프로그램을 알고 싶습니다.

　 I'd like to know the programs and schedules of movies today at the Village Theater.

B: 영화는 10시에 시작될 것입니다. 그리고 한국 음식축제는 11시에 열릴 것입니다.

　 The movies will be shown at 10:00, and the Korean Food festival will take place at 11:00.

A: 오늘 세종문화센터에서 어떤 공연이 있나요?

　 Is there any performance at Sejong Cultural Center today?

B: 네, 현대무용공연이 10시에 있습니다.

　 Yes, there will be a Modern Dance performance at 10:00.

A: 여기에서 가까운 카톨릭 교회는 어디 있나요?

　 Where is the Catholic church near here?

B: 오륜여자중학교 주위에 위치해 있습니다.

　 It is located near the Oryun Girls' Middle School.

A: 저에게 내일 날씨상태; 기온, 풍향, 풍속을 알려주시겠어요?

　 Could you tell me the weather condition, the temperature, the direction, and velocity of wind tomorrow?

B: 내일은 다소 맑고 기온은 최고 10도 최저 3로 예상되겠습니다. 바람은 시속 2km로 동남풍이 불겠습니다.

IV. Attendance in the Olympics

It will be more or less clear tomorrow, and the expected temperature is between 3 and 10 degrees Celsius. The wind will blow southeast at the speed of 2 kilometers per hour.

A: 영국 대사관이 어딘지 알려주시겠어요?
Could you tell me where the British Embassy is?

B: 영국대사관은 시청에서 가깝고 덕수궁 정문 바로 오른쪽에 위치해 있습니다.
The British Embassy is located near the City Hall and just on the right of Deoksoo Palace's main gate.

A: 올림픽 선수촌에서 어디로 가면 영자신문을 살 수 있나요?
Where can I buy an English-language newspaper in the Olympic Village?

B: 올림픽 선수촌 쇼핑센터 안의 신문과 잡지 판매대에서 살 수 있습니다.
You can buy it at the newspaper and magazine stand inside the Village Shopping Center.

A: 가정방문프로그램을 신청할 방법을 알려주세요. 또한 이 프로그램의 출발 시간과 장소도 알려주세요.
Please tell me how to apply for the Home Visit Program, and also the time and place of departure for this program.

B: 가정방문프로그램을 위한 신청자들은 선착순으로 접수됩니다. 그리고 출발은 선수홀 앞쪽의 국기광장에서 10시입니다.
Requests for the Home Visit Program are accepted on a first-come first-served basis. And the departure is at the Flag Plaza in front of the Athletes' Hall at 10:00.

A: 산업체 투어프로그램에 대해 말해 주십시오.
Please tell me something about the Industrial TourProgram.

B: 산업체 시설과 관광지를 연결하는 몇몇의 산업체 체험 코스가 있습니다. 투

IV. Attendance in the Olympics

어는 무료입니다. 당신은 안내센터에서 요청하면 됩니다. 신청자들은 등록 접수 순서이며 출발은 선수홀 앞입니다.

There are several courses of the Industry Tour Program, which link industrial facilities with tourist spots. The tour is offered without charge. You may request it at the Information Center. Requests are accepted in the order of registration, and departures are in front of the Athletes' Hall.

B: 이 편지를 A4용지로 10장 복사해 주시겠어요?

Could you make 10 copies of this letter in A4 size?

A: 네, 잠시만 기다리세요. 비용은 1만원입니다. 은행에 지불해 주세요.

Yes, please wait for a moment. The cost is 10,000 won. Please pay the amount at the bank.

B: 이 초대장을 영어로 번역해 주세요.

Please translate this letter of invitation into English.

A: 알겠습니다. 내일 오후 6시에 이것을 찾으러 오세요. 비용은 100,000원입니다. 그리고 당신은 은행에 지불하셔야 합니다. 만일 그것에 관련하여 질문이 있으면, 당신의 대표단사무실에 연락하겠습니다.

All right. Come back for it by 6 p.m. tomorrow. It costs 100,000 won, and you may pay at the bank. If there are any questions related to it, we will get in touch with your delegation office.

B: 저는 정원 약 500명 수용 좌석을 가진 회의실 사용을 신청하고 싶습니다.

I want to apply for the use of a conference room with a seating capacity of about 500 people.

A: 알겠습니다. 당신의 이름과 아파트 호실을 남기고 가세요. 오후 6시까지 방 배정(회의실)을 알려드리겠습니다.

I see. Please leave your name and apartment unit number. I will inform you of the room assignment by 6 p.m.

Ⅳ. Attendance in the Olympics

B: 저희는 냉장고 2대를 빌리고 싶어요.

We would like to rent 2 refrigerators.

A: 좋습니다, 몇 분만 기다려주시겠어요? 임대료는 150,000원 이고 은행에 지불해주세요. 그들은 당신이 원하는 곳에 설치해드릴 것입니다.

All right, will you please wait for a minute? The rental fee is 150,000 won, and pay the amount at the bank. They will be installed where you want.

6. International Cooperation
(국제협력)

A: 기술위원회미팅 회의실이 어디에 있습니까?

Where is the conference room for the Technical Committee meeting?

B: 회의실은 선수 홀의 2층 2호실입니다.

It is conference room No. 2 on the 2nd floor of the Athletes' Hall.

A: 언제 회의가 시작 되나요?

When does the conference begin?

B: 8시에 시작합니다.

It begins at 8 o'clock.

A: 나는 국제협력 담당자와 의논할 게 있습니다.

I have something to discuss with the manager incharge of the International Cooperation.

B: 무엇에 관한 것인지 물어봐도 될까요?(무엇 때문입니까?)

May I ask what it is about?

A: 우리는 매니저와 의논(상담)해서 시간과 장소를 정할 것입니다.

We will consult the manager and fix the time and the place.

B: 그를 언제 그를 만나길 원하십니까?

When do you want to see him?

A: 그 문제에 관해선, 담당 매니저와 상담하세요.

On that matter, you'd better consult the manager in charge.

B: 급히 프랑스어 통역원이 필요합니다.

IV. Attendance in the Olympics

I need someone to interpret French urgently.

A: 얼마 동안 그가 필요하십니까?
How long do you need him?

B: 어디, 그리고 누구에게 그를 보내면 될까요?
Where and to whom shall I send him?

A: 무엇 때문에 통역원이 필요합니까?
What do you need the interpreter for?

B: 공교롭게도 우리는 지금 당장 이용할 수 있는 다른 프랑스어 통역원이 없습니다.
It so happens that we don't have another French language interpreter available right now.

A: 그가 할 형편이 되면, 나는 즉시 당신에게 알릴 것입니다.
When he is available, I will let you know immediately.

B: 제가 어디로 연락드리면 될까요?
Where can I contact you?

A: 이와 같은 일이 당신에게 불편을 초래해서 죄송합니다. 우리는 그것을 시정할 것이며, 이와 같은 일 다시는 일어나지 않을 것을 보장합니다.
I am very sorry that something like this has caused you an inconvenience. We will correct it, and ensure that it will not happen again.

B: 누군가에게 늦지 않도록 주의를 촉구할 때.
When calling someone's attention so that he may not be late.

A: 행사가 시장 없이 시행되도록 세 시간에 오세요(시산을 지켜라).
Please be on time, so that the ceremony may be carried out without difficulty.

Ⅳ. Attendance in the Olympics

7. The Flag Raising Ceremony
(국기 게양식)

1) Requesting for a conversation concerning the ceremony
(행사와 관련된 대화 요구하기)

1-1   처음 뵙겠습니다. 저는 올림픽 선수촌에서 행사를 담당하는 매니저입니다.
How do you do? I am the manager in charge of the ceremony in the Olympic Village.

1-2   저는 당신의 국기게양식과 관련해 단장과 대화하고 싶습니다. (단장이 없음)
I'd like to talk to your Chef de Mission concerning your Flag Raising Ceremony.(When the Chef de Mission is absent.)

1-3   음, 그러면 부단장이나 다른 팀 임원과 이야기할 수 있을까요? (그들 모두 없다).
Well, then, may I talk to the Assistant Chef de Mission or any other team official?(When all of them are absent.)

1-4   그렇다면, 나중에 연락하겠습니다. 하지만 누군가(그들 중) 일찍 돌아오면, 나에게 연락하도록 해주세요. 나의 사무실 전화번호는 750-5213입니다. (대표자 또는 관계자가 가능할 때)
In that case, I will call back later, but when someone returns early, will you please have him call me at my office? My office number is 750-5213.(When the Chef de Mission or a team official is available.)

1-5   처음 뵙겠습니다. 올림픽 선수촌에 방문하신 것을 환영합니다. 나는 Mr. Park이고, 국기게양식을 담당하는 매니저입니다. 우리는 입실한 다음

IV. Attendance in the Olympics

날 각 대표단의 행사를 열기로 결정하였습니다. 그러므로 우리는 내일 입실 행사를 하고자 합니다. 저는 당신이 매우 바쁘다는 것을 알지만, 나의 사무실에서 자세한 내용을 당신과 상의하고 싶습니다. 우리는 아침 10시경에 만날 수 있을까요?

How do you do? Welcome to the Olympic Village. I am Mr. Park, manager in charge of the flag raising ceremony. We have decided to hold the ceremony for each delegation the day after their actual check-in. Therefore, we want to hold your check-in ceremony tomorrow. I know you are very busy, but I wish to discuss the details with you at my office. Could we meet around 10 o'clock in the morning?

1-6 미안하지만, 그때 다른 대표단과의 약속이 이미 잡혀있습니다. 한 시간 일찍(늦게) 할 수 있을까요?

I am sorry, but an appointment with another delegation has already been scheduled at that time. Can we make it an hour earlier (or later)?

1-7 좋아요, 나의 사무실에서 10시에 기다리겠습니다. 나의 사무실은 주 도로로부터 올림픽 선수촌 국기 광장 입구의 오른쪽에 있는 선수홀의 1층 맨 끝에 위치하고 있습니다. 궁금하신 일이 있으면, 행사 사무소 전화번호는 616-3400입니다.

Good, I will wait for you at 10 o'clock in my office. My office is located at the far end of the first floor of the Athletes' Hall at the right hand side of the entrance toward the Olympic Village flag plaza from the main road. For your information, the Ceremony Office number is 616-3400.

2) Discussing the Flag Raising Ceremony
(국기 계양식에 대해 논의하기)

2-1 만나 뵙게 되어 영광입니다. 저는 국기 계양식을 담당하고 있는 Mr.

Ⅳ. Attendance in the Olympics

Park입니다. 첫 번째, 시간에 관해 당신의 요청서에 의하면, 당신은 10시를 원합니다. 우리도 좋습니다.

I am glad to meet you. I am Mr. Park, in charge of the flag raising ceremony. First, about the time. According to your request form, you want 10:00. It is all right with us, too.

2-2 　당신의 요청서에 따르면, 10시인데, 그 시간에 이미 다른 행사가 예정되었습니다.

According to your request form, you want 10:00. but another ceremony has already been scheduled at that time.

2-3 　보통, 당신의 대표단이 매우 크기 때문에 5국가의 행사가 동시에 이루어집니다.

Usually, the ceremony is to be held for 5 countries at the same time because your delegation is very large.

2-4 　내일 아침 10시에 하기를 제안합니다. 괜찮습니까?

I suggest 10 a.m. tomorrow. Is it all right with you?

2-5 　글쎄요, 당신 국가와 동시에 식을 하는 국가는 일본과 대만입니다.

Let's see. The countries holding the ceremony concurrently with you are Japan and Taiwan.

2-6 　당신의 바람을 충분히 이해하지만 우리의 방침과 사정상 한 번에 한 국가 행사를 개최하기가 불가능합니다. 알다시피, 우리는 5일 이내에 167개국의 행사를 개최해야 합니다. 여태까지 단지 10개국만 행사를 하였습니다. 우리의 입장을 이해주셨으면 합니다.

I fully understand your wish, but in view of our policy and the circumstances, it is not possible to hold the ceremony for a single nation at a time. As you know, we have to hold ceremonies for 167 countries within 5 days, and so far we have been able to hold them only for 10 countries. I hope you will understand our position.

2-7 행사에 당신이 초대하고 싶은 사람이 있으면 신청서에 그들의 이름을 쓰십시오. 숙소에 돌아가면 신청서 자세히 작성하셔서, 통역요원에게 오늘 10시까지 NOC서비스센터에 제출하게 해주십시오. 한 장에 한 사람만입니다.

If there's anyone you want to invite to the ceremony, please write their names on this application form. When you go back to your lodging fill out the form in details, and have your interpreter submit it to the NOC service center by 10 o'clock today. One form is for one person only.

2-8 지금 당신의 국기와 국가를 점검해 주시겠습니까? 그것들에 아무 문제가 없다고 믿습니다. 상당항 주의를 기울여 주의 깊게 점검했습니다. 점검을 하셨으면 이 신청서에 사인해 주십시오.

Now will you please check your national flag and national anthem? I believe there is nothing wrong with them. We have paid considerable attention and checked it carefully. Please sign on the application form, if you have.

2-9 올림픽 선수촌장이 행사 중에 단장에게 기념품을 증정할 것입니다. 당신의 선수단도 준비한 게 있으면, 기념품을 상호 교환하고 싶습니다.

The Mayor of the Olympic Village will present a souvenir to the Chef de Mission during the ceremony. If your delegation has prepared something, we would like to exchange souvenirs.

2-10 행사에서는 한국어뿐만 아니라 올림픽 공식언어인 영어와 불어가 사용될 것입니다.

English and French, the Olympic official languages, as well as Korean language will be used in the ceremony.

2-11 그러나 당신과 함께 행사에 참가하는 모든 나라가 당신과 같은 언어를

Ⅳ. Attendance in the Olympics

말하기 때문에, 행사중 당신의 언어를 사용할 것을 고려할 것입니다.
However, since all the countries attending the ceremony together speak the same language as you, we will consider using your language during the ceremony.

2-12 그렇다면, 당신의 파견단 소속 통역원 중 1명이 식을 속행할 것입니다.
In that case, one of the interpreters dispatched to your delegation will expedite the ceremony.

2-13 당신의 행사에서, 아랍 언어를 사용하는 중동 국가가 포함되어 있습니다. 그래서, 우리는 공식 언어중 하나로 식을 개최할 것입니다.
In your ceremony, one Middle East nation which uses Arabic language is included. So, we will hold it with one of the official languages.

2-14 행사를 하는 동안, 올림픽촌장이 환영사를 할 것입니다. 그러나 단장은 답사를 할 필요가 없습니다. 몇 개국이 행사에 관여되었기에 답사 없이 하기로 결정했습니다.
During the ceremony, the Mayor of the Olympic Village will make a welcoming speech, but the Chef de Mission need not make a reply. We have decided to go without it, because several countries are involved in a ceremony.

2-15 우리는 다양한 방법으로 파견단을 균등한 분배나 투숙을 기대했습니다. 그러나 현재 파견단이 투숙하기 위해 밀려드니, 단장이 아직 체크인 하지 않았지만 누군가가 단장을 대신해서 파견단의 일부와 행사를 갖기로 했습니다.
We have expected the equal distribution in equal distribution in various ways. But when the delegations swarm to check in as now, we have decided to have the ceremony with only a part of the delegation even if its Chef de Mission has not checked in yet and someone can fill in on his behalf. I hope you will understand.

2-16 행사 후에, 대표단과 올림픽촌의 임원들이 서로 알 수 있도록 간단한 환영파티를 준비했습니다.

Following the ceremony, we have arranged a brief welcoming party so that the delegations and the officials of the Olympic Village may get to know one another.

2-17 이제 행사 날짜와 절차에 대해 이야기를 끝마쳤으므로, 행사의 실질적인 조치를 취하겠습니다. 그렇게 하기 전에, 어떤 특별한 요구나 질문이 있습니까?

Now that we have completed our talk on the date and procedure of the ceremony, we will turn to the practical steps of the ceremony. Before doing so, do you have any special demands or questions?

3) Procedure of the ceremony (행사절차)

3-1 제가 행사의 자세한 과정을 설명해 드리겠습니다. 가지고 있는 종이를 참조해 주세요.

I will explain the detailed process of the ceremony. Please refer to the program you have.

3-2 우리의 행사요원이 당신의 단장님을 안내해 드릴 목적으로 행사 20분 전에 숙소로 갈 것입니다.

One of our ceremony staff will come to your lodging 20 minutes before the ceremony for purpose of escorting your Chef de Mission.

3-3 단장님은 그와(행사요원) 함께 시장실로 가시기 바랍니다. 그곳에서 상호간에 인사와 간단한 대화를 나누고, 그리고 행사 시작 5분 전에 행사장으로 떠날 것입니다.

The Chef de Mission is asked to come to the Mayor's office with him. There, they will be introduced each other, have a brief chat and leave for the ceremony 5 minutes before it begins.

Ⅳ. Attendance in the Olympics

3-4 어디에서, 어떻게 그가 사장님하고 같이 떠날 지는 촌장실에서 설명드릴 것입니다.

From where and how he is to leave with the Mayor will be explained in the Mayor's office.

3-5 당신의 국기를 선수촌장실에서 전달받고 당신의 선수들 중 한 명이 그것을 행사장으로 가져갈 것입니다. 그러므로 당신이 선수촌장실에 갈 때 선수를 데리고 가야합니다.

Your national flag will be delivered at the Mayor's office and one of your athletes will carry it to the ceremonial place. Therefore you should take an athlete with you when you go to the Mayor's office.

3-6 선수촌장님, 단장님, 참석자들이 도착해 단상(플랫폼)에 오르고, 기수(국기든 선수)가 그의 대표단 앞으로 이동하고, 나머지 참가자들이 예정된 자리를 취하면 행사가 시작됩니다. (☞ vip가 무대에 자리하고 각 나라별로 국기 들고 정렬한 상태를 말합니다. 그리고 안내원이 각 나라별로 서 있는 장면임).

The ceremony begins when the Mayor and the Chef de Mission and attendants arrive and go up to the platform, the flag-carrying athlete moves to the front of his delegation, and the rest of the attendants occupy their pre-arranged positions.

3-7 행사를 하는 동안, 기를 운반하는 선수는 국기게양대로 걸어 나가 우리의 기수(flagmen)에게 건네주고, '국기게양' 순서에 따라 국기가 게양되면 그가 원래 있던 자리로 되돌아옵니다.

During the ceremony, the flag-carrying athlete will walk toward the flag stand, hand the flag over to our flagmen, and then return to his original position after the flag is raised according to the 'Flag Hoisting' procedure.

3-8 행사 15분 전, 피켓 멤버가 당신의 대표단을 이끌기 위해 숙소에 도착할

IV. Attendance in the Olympics

것입니다. 그러므로 행사에 참가하는 대표단은 숙소의 광장에 줄을 서서 피켓멤버의 인도로 행사장으로 출발합니다. 각 대표단은 4열로 정렬하지만 상황에 배열은 조절될 수 있습니다.

Fifteen minutes before the ceremony, the picket member will arrive at your lodgings to lead your delegation. Therefore, the delegation participating in the ceremony is to line up at the plaza of the lodgings and start for the ceremonial place by the lead of the picket member. Each delegation is to line up in 4 lines, but the arrangement can be adjusted depending on the circumstances.

3-9 이것이 행사의 절차에 대해 제가 말해야 하는 모든 것입니다. 질문 있으십니까?

This is all that I have to say on the process of the ceremony. Do you have any questions?

3-10 바쁘신 일정에도 불구하고 들어주신 당신의 인내에 감사드립니다. 당신의 대표단에 행운이 있기를 바랍니다. 내일 뵙겠습니다.

We appreciate your patience in listening in spite of your busy schedule. I wish your delegation a good luck, and I will see you tomorrow.

Ⅳ. Attendance in the Olympics

8. Meal Service
(식사 서비스)

A: 제가 점심도시락을 언제, 어디에서 주문할 수 있는지 알려주시겠어요?
Could you tell me when and where I could apply for a box lunch?

B: 당신이 점심도시락이 필요하기 전날 아침 7시에서 9시 사이에 NOC서비스센터에 있는 도시락부서에 당신의 단장 이름으로 요청(주문)할 수 있습니다.
You can request at the Box Lunch Desk in the NOC Service Center between 7 a.m. and 9 a.m. the day before you need them in the name of your Chef de Mission.

A: 점심도시락의 메뉴는 무엇인가요?
What is the menu of the box lunch?

B: 저희는 5일주기의 표준 메뉴를 제공하고 있지만 특별한 주문에 따라 준비되어지기도 합니다. 이것은 주로 2,500칼로리를 포함하는 샌드위치로 이루어져있습니다.
We gave the standard menu of a 5-day cycle, but it can also be prepared on your special request. It is mainly made up of sandwiches with 2,500 calories.

A: 제가 직접 점심을 가져가야 되나요?
May I take the box lunch myself?

B: 아니요, 점심도시락은 올림픽 선수촌의 주방에서 점심 도시락 메이커에 의해 준비되어지고, 당신이 작성한 신청서에 표현한 장소와 시간에 냉장 운반차로 운반되어 집니다. 당신을 위해 편의점 직원이이 도시락을 보관할 것입니다.

IV. Attendance in the Olympics

No, they are prepared by the box lunch makers in the dining hall of the Olympic Village, delivered by a refrigerator van to the place and at the hour you requested in the application form. The staff of a convenience store will keep them for you.

A: 저는 오늘의 메뉴를 좋아하지 않습니다. 다른 메뉴를 가져다주시겠어요?

I don't like today's menu. May I have another menu?

B: 그렇다면, 당신은 5일주기의 표준메뉴 중 어느 하나를 고를 수 있습니다. 또는 당신이 주문서에 특별한 요구를 한다면, 우리는 그에 맞춰서 특별한 점심 도시락을 만들 것입니다.

You, in that case, you may choose any one out of the standard menu of a 5-day cycle. Or if you state a special demand in your request form we will make a special box lunch accordingly.

A: 단지 점심만 도시락으로 제공되나요?

Is the box lunch offered only for lunch?

B: 아니요, 저녁도 역시 준비될 수 있습니다.

No, it can also be prepared for the evening.

Ⅳ. Attendance in the Olympics

9. The Amenities
(편의시설)

1) Telecommunications Service Center (통신서비스 센터)

1-1 안녕하세요. 여기서 저희는 해외 통신선과 전화를 다루고 있습니다.
Hello. Here we handle overseas cables and telephones.

1-2 무엇을 도와드릴까요?
What can I do for you?

1-3 여기 케이블 (신청)작성지가 있습니다. 이것을 채워주시겠어요? 케이블 비용은 20,000원입니다.
Here is a cable form. Will you please fill it out? The cable charge is 20,000 won.

1-4 여기 통신 신청서가 있습니다. 이것을 채워주시겠어요?
Here is a telecommunication form. Will you please fill it out?

1-5 Mr. Kim, 당신의 해외전화는 지금 개통(준비)되었습니다. 전화기박스의 No. 3을 사용해주세요. 당신은 전화통화를 끝냈습니까? 비용은 5,000원입니다.
Mr. Kim, your overseas call is now ready. Please use telephone box No. 3. Have you finished your call? The charge is 5,000 won.

2) Post Office (우체국)

2-1 안녕하세요. 여기서 저희는 일반 우편과 우편소포를 다루고 있습니다. 무엇을 도와드릴까요?

Hello. Here we handle the general mail and parcel post. What can I do for you?

2-2   우편을 위한 우편요금은 1,500원입니다.
The postage for this mail is 1,500 won.

2-3   저희는 여기에서 당신의 소포를 포장해드릴 수 있습니다. 포장비용은 1,000원 입니다.
We can wrap your parcel here. The wrapping charge is 1,000 won.

2-4   저희는 기념우표와 엽서를 팝니다. 또한 기념우표 책도 팝니다. 둘러보시겠습니까?
We sell commemorative stamps and postcards. We also sell commemorative stamp books. Would you like to take a look?

2-5   이 우표들은 250원입니다.
These stamps cost 250 won.

2-6   이것은 당신의 우편환의 합계입니다. 확인하시겠습니까?
This is the amount of cash for your postal money order. Will you please confirm?

3) Shopping Center (쇼핑센터)

A: 안녕하세요, 여기는 쇼핑센터입니다.
Hello, this is the shopping center.

B: 당신을 위해 우리가 무엇을 도와드릴까요?
What can we do for you?

A: 무엇보다도 우리는 서울 올림픽경기를 기념하는 기념품들을 가지고 있습니다. 예를 들어 상징물, 호돌이 배지, 공식 마스코트, 열쇠고리, 그리고 수저 세트입니다. 게다가, 옷감, 생활필수품, 의류, 화장품, 액세서리, 전자제품,

Ⅳ. Attendance in the Olympics

그리고 음식과 같은 올림픽 선수촌에서 선택된 물건들이 있습니다.

We have, most of all, souvenirs commemorating the Seoul Olympic Games. For example, emblems, badges bearing Hodori, the official mascot, key holders, and spoon sets. Besides, there are goods selected for shopping in Olympic Village, such as textile goods, daily necessities, clothing, cosmetics, accessories, electronic goods, and some food.

B: 저는 한국의 상징적인 것을 사고 싶습니다.

I want to buy something symbolic of Korea.

A: 전통공예품/코너는 롯데 백화점입니다. 한국 조상의 정신을 담고(구체화) 있는 청·백도자기들, 목제 조각품, 그리고 칠기(류)가 있습니다.

The traditional arts-crafts corner is at Lotte Department Store. There are blue and white ceramics, wood carvings, and lacquer-wares, which embody the Korean ancestral spirit.

B: 면세코너가 있습니까?

there a duty-free corner?

A: 네, 있습니다. 그곳에서 그들은 전기제품, 의류, 옷감, 액세서리, 담배, 향수 등을 팝니다. 저희는 당신의 편의를 위해, 물건하나당 100달러미만인 상품과 개인당 1,000 달러미만인 사람들에 한에 특별하게 공항 픽럽대에서 직접 찾아가는 것 대신에 매장 진열대에서 가져가는 것을 허용합니다. (☞ 매장에서 산 물건을 맡기고 공항 픽업대에서 찾아가는 것이 아니라 산 물건을 직접 가져가는 것을 말함.)

Yes, there is. There they sell electrical goods, clothing, textile goods, accessories, tobacco, perfume, etc. We especially allow over-the-counter deliveries, instead of airport pick-up, for merchandise worth less than $100 per item and less than 1,000 per person, for your convenience.

B: 이것은 얼마입니까?

How much is this?

A: 이것은 110,000원이고 미화 100달러입니다.
It is 110,00 won, $100 in US dollars.

B: 여기에 어느 국가화폐를 받습니까?
Which national currencies are accepted here?

A: 저희는 오직 원화나, 미화 그리고 비자카드만 받습니다.
We only accept Korean won, US dollars and VISA card.

B: 저는 여기보단 더 크고 다양한 물건이 있는 장소에서 쇼핑하고 싶습니다. 갈 수 있나요?
I would like to do some shopping in a place where there are a greater variety of goods than here. Where can I go?

A: 오, 당신은 롯데백화점에서 품질이 좋은 인삼제품을 구할 것입니다.
Oh, you will find a high quality ginseng products at Lotte Department Store.

4) Coffee / Music Room (커피 / 음악 방)

A: 이곳은 커피 / 음악 방입니다.
This is a coffee/music room.

B: 어떤 종류의 차를 좋아하나요?
What kind of tea would you like?

A: 우리는 녹차 종류의 차를 제공하는데 공짜입니다. 당신은 여기서 아무 때나 차와 음악을 즐기며 긴장을 풀 수가 있습니다.
We serve many kinds of green tea and they are free of charge. You can relax here enjoying the tea and music at any time. Self-service is the rule here.

B: 저희가 특별한 음악을 신청해도 될까요?
May we request a special piece of music?

Ⅳ. Attendance in the Olympics

A: 네, 여기 신청서가 있습니다. 그리고 당신이 원한다면 여기에서 장기, 바둑, 또는 체스와 같은 게임을 할 수가 있습니다. 또한 선반에 있는 신문과 잡지를 자유롭게 읽을 수도 있습니다.(그들이 원래 있던 곳에) 잡지를 제자리에 갖다 놓으세요.
Yes, this is a request form. And you may play games such as Janggi, Badook or chess here, if you wish. You may also freely read newspapers and magazines in the rack. Please put magazines back where they were.

5) Barber Shop/ Beauty Salon (이발소/미장원)

A: 안녕하세요. 이곳은 이발소입니다. 머리를 어떻게 해드릴까요?
Hello, this is the barber shop. How do you want your hair done?

B: 당신은 어떤 종류의 서비스를 제공하죠?
What kind of services do you offer?

A: 헤어컷, 면도, 머리 말리기, 그리고 샴푸를 합니다.
Haircut, shaving, hair dry, and shampoo.

B: 서비스가 공짜인가요? 아님 돈을 받나요?
Is the service free, or do you charge?

A: 우리는 돈을 받지만 서비스는 비영리원칙으로 가능한 최소의 비용으로 제공되어 집니다. 헤어 컷 서비스의 가격은 10,000원입니다.
We charge, but the service is provided at the lowest cost possible on a non-profit basis. The price of hair-cut service is 10,000 won.

B: 어떤 지폐(통화)를 받습니까? (어느 나라 돈)
What currency do you accept?

A: 저희는 규칙으로 원화를 받습니다. 만일 다른 지폐를 가지고 계신다면, 첫 번째 층에 있는 은행에서 원화로 교환해야 합니다.
We accept the Korean won as a rule. If you have any other currency, you

IV. Attendance in the Olympics

may exchange it for won at the bank on the first floor.

B: 여기 헤어살롱에서 어떤 종류의 서비스를 받을 수 있을까요?

What kind of service can I get at this hair salon?

A: 헤어 컷과 드라이, 샴푸, 메이크업, 매니큐어, 페디큐어, 파마, 그리고 염색이 있습니다. 당신의 헤어스타일을 어떻게 해드리면 될까요? 이런 종류의 헤어스타일을 좋아하시나요?

Haircut and dry, shampoo, make-up, manicure, pedicure, permanent, and dyeing. How do you want your hair style done? Do you like this kind of hair style?

B: 네, 여기에서 당신이 사용하는 제품들을 살 수 있을까요?

Yes. Can I buy the products you are using here?

A: 저희는 여기에서 그것들을 팔지 않습니다. 하지만 우리 옆집인 쇼핑센터의 화장품코너에서 그것들을 찾을 수 있을 겁니다.

We do not sell them here. But you may find them in the cosmetics corner of the shopping center next to us.

6) Discotheque (디스코텍)

A: 그 디스코텍은 언제 오픈 하나요?

When does the discotheque open?

B: 오후 6시부터 오후 10시까지 입니다.

It is open from 6 p.m. to 10 p.m.

A: 우리가 좋아하는 음악을 신청할 수 있나요?

Can we request our favorite music?

B: 네, 신청서를 작성하시고 웨이터(웨이트리스)한테 주세요.

Yes, you may fill out a request form and hand it over to a waiter(waitress).

Ⅳ. Attendance in the Olympics

A: 디스코 대회가 있나요?
  Is there a disco competition?

B: 네, 일주일에 한 번 있습니다.
  Yes, there is once a week.

A: 대회에서 우승하면 상을 주나요?
  Is any prize given to a winner in the competition?

B: 네, 물론이죠.
  Yes, of course.

A: 어떻게 대회에 참가할 수 있나요?
  How can we participate in the competition?

B: 신청서를 작성하시고 대회하기 2일 전에 디스코텍의 매니저한테 주어야합니다.
  You may fill out an application form and give it to the management personnel of the discotheque 2 days before the competition.

A: 어디에서 음료수 좀 마실 수 있나요?
  Where can I get some soft drinks?

B: 당신 저기에서 아무 때나(언제든지) 마실 수 있습니다.
  You can get some over there at any time.

A: 디스코텍에는 밴드가 없나요?
  Isn't there a band in the discotheque?

B: 네, 없습니다.
  No, there is not.

7) Laundry Shop (세탁소)

A: 여기는 세탁소입니다. 저희가 제공하는 서비스의 종류와 가격이 어떻게 되

는지 알고 싶다면 가격표를 보세요.

This is the laundry. Please look over the price list if you want to know what kinds of service we offer and what the costs are.

B: 세탁물을 좀 가지고 왔어요. 제가 어떻게 하면 되나요?

I have brought some laundry. What should I do?

A: 당신이 원하는 서비스가 무엇인지 말씀해주세요. 저희는 당신의 요청에 따라 행동할겁니다. 그리고 찾으러 오실 때 이 영수증을 함께 가지고 오세요. 저희는 오직 원화만 받습니다.

Please tell me what service you want. We will act according to your request. And come back with this receipt to get it back. We only accept Korean won.

B: 당신은 세탁물을 룸 서비스 해주십니까?

Can you do room service for laundry?

A: 아니요, 당신이 직접 우리에게서 찾아서(골라내서) 가져가야 합니다.

No, you must bring it to us and pick it up yourself.

8) Art Studio (공방)

8-1   이곳은 공방입니다.

This is an art studio.

8-2   저희는 즉석에서 당신의 초상화를 그립니다.

We draw your own portrait on the spot.

8-3   잠깐 들르셔서 당신에게 잘 맞는 스타일이 어느 것인지 골라주세요.

Please come over and choose a style that suits you.

8-4   앉아주세요.

Please be seated.

IV. Attendance in the Olympics

8-5 가격은 5,000원이고 저희는 오직 원화만 받습니다.

The price is 5,000 won, and we only accept Korean won.

8-6 이 그림들은 한국 풍경의 삽화입니다.

These pictures are illustrations of the Korean landscape.

9) After Service / Repair Shop (애프터 서비스 / 수리점)

A: (당신은) 여기에선 무엇을 합니까?

What do you do here?

B: 저희는 옷, 가방, 서류가방, 슈트가방, 신발 등을 수리하고 또한 마사지 서비스를 제공하고 있습니다.

We repair clothes, bags, briefcases, suitcases, shoes, etc. and also offer a massage service.

A: 얼마 받습니까?

How much do you charge?

B: 서비스는 공짜입니다.

The service is free.

A: 어떻게 해야 마사지를 받습니까?

How can I get a massage?

B: 당신은 하루전날에 마사지직원한테 부탁할 수 있습니다.

You can request the management staff one day inadvance.

A: 당신은 저기에서 신청서를 찾을 수 있을 것입니다.

You will find a request form there.

B: 여기서 물건을 좀 살 수 있습니까?

Can I buy some goods here?

A: 저희는 팔지 않습니다. 하지만 쇼핑센터에서 찾을 수 있을 것입니다.

We do not sell them here. But you will find them in the shopping center.

10) Photo Studio (사진관)

A: (당신은) 여기에서 주로 무엇을 합니까?

What do you do here mainly?

B: 저희는 증명사진과 명함사진, 또 다른 사이즈의 사진을 찍습니다.

We take photos for ID cards, those of a name-card size, and all other sizes.

A: 언제 제 사진을 찾아가면 될까요?

When can I pick up my photos?

B: 2일 후에 오세요.

Please come back 2 days later.

A: 얼마입니까?

How much is it?

B: 가격표가 여기 있습니다.

Here is the price list.

A: 사진을 찍기 위해 다른 장소로 갈수 있습니까?

Can you go to other places to take photographs?

B: 네, 갈 수 있습니다.

Yes, you can.

A: 원본 필름을 줄 수 있나요?

Do you give me the original film?

B: 네, 줄 수 있습니다.

Yes, we do.

Ⅳ. Attendance in the Olympics

11) Korean Pavilion (한국관)

11-1   이곳은 한국관입니다.
       This is the Korean Pavilion.

11-2   여기에서, 저희는 다양한 한국의 국보와 전통문화상, 한국의 발전(모습)을 보여주고 있습니다.
       Here, we show the various Korean national treasures, and features of traditional culture and of Korea's development.

11-3   당신이 원한다면 관광과 티켓서비스에 관해 조언을 제공합니다.
       We also offer suggestions on sightseeing and a ticketing service, if you wish.

12) Movie Theater (극장)

12-1   이곳은 극장이고, 저희는 또한 다른 종류의 연극을 상영합니다.
       This is a movie theater, and we also stage shows of different kinds.

12-2   입장료가 없습니다.
       There is no entrance charge.

12-3   저희는 하루에 2번 영화를 상영하는데 각각 오후 3시~5시와 오후 8시~10(입니다.)
       We show movies twice a day, between 3 p.m. and 5 p.m. and between 8 p.m. and 10 p.m., respectively.

12-4   영화 상영과 연극 공연이 사전에 올림픽 선수촌의 게시판 포스터에 의해 알려지게 될 것입니다.
       Movie showings and stage performances will be announced in advance by posters on the bulletin board of the Olympic Village.

12-5   영화는 주로 한국 드라마, 그리고 전통적인 한국 문화와 예술의 단편일

IV. Attendance in the Olympics

것입니다.

The films will be mainly Korean dramas, and cultural pieces showing traditional Korean culture and art.

12-6 저희는 선수들이 참가하는 프로그램을 가질 것이며 그리고 일부 다른 작은(공연)이 매일 오후 8시에서 오후 10시에 상영합니다. 그리고 저희는 매일 그 쇼를 바꿀 것입니다.

We will have programs in which athletes take part, and some other small shows every day between 8 p.m. and 10 p.m., and we will change them each day.

13) Outdoor Performance Stage (야외 공연 무대)

13-1 야외 공연은 계속해서 16일 동안 열릴 것이고, 또한 올림픽선수촌의 오프닝 전날 밤 축제와 함께 시작됩니다. 기간은 9월 16일에서 10월 1일 고별 무대의 밤까지.

The outdoor performances will take place continuously for 16 days, beginning with the festival on the night before the opening of the Olympic Village on September 16 until the farewell party on the night of October 1.

13-2 야외 공연은 입장료가 없습니다.(무료입니다)

The outdoor performances are free of charge.

13-3 공연은 한국의 인기가요, 서양 팝 음악, 디스코 댄스, 한국 전통춤, 한국 고전희가극, 패션쇼, 기타 등등으로 구성되었는데, 한국에 대해 많은 것을 배우는 데 도움이 될 것입니다.

The performances consist of Korean popular songs, western pop music, disco dance, Korean traditional dance, Korean classical music comedy, fashion shows, etc.⋯, which will help you learn much about Korea.

Ⅳ. Attendance in the Olympics

14) Billiards Room (당구장)

A: 안녕하세요, 여기는 당구장입니다.
   Hello, this is the billiards room.

B: 저희는 당구를 치고 싶습니다. 장비를 빌릴 수 있을까요?
   We want to play billiards. May we borrow the equipment?

A: 물론이죠, 포볼 아니면 로테이션으로 하시겠습니까?
   Yes. Is it a four ball, or is it rotation pool?

B: 포볼요.
   Four ball, please.

A: 여기 볼이 있습니다. 당신은 큐 박스에서 큐를 찾을 수 있습니다.
   Here are the balls. You will find cues in the cue box.

15) Table Tennis Room (탁구장)

A: 안녕하세요, 여기는 탁구장입니다.
   Hello, this is the table tennis room.

B: 탁구를 치고 싶습니다. 장비를 빌릴 수 있을까요?
   We want to play table tennis. May we borrow equipment?

A: 단식 아니면 복식하실 겁니까?
   Is it for singles or doubles?

B: 복식요.
   It is for doubles.

A: 여기 라켓과 볼이 있습니다. No. 1 테이블(탁구대)을 사용해주세요.
   Here are rackets and balls. Please use Table No. 1.

IV. Attendance in the Olympics

16) Video Game Room (비디오게임장)

16-1 안녕하세요, 여기는 비디오게임장입니다.
Hello, this is the video game room.

16-2 당신은 무료로 게임을 즐길 수 있습니다.
You may enjoy the game free of charge.

16-3 게임을 하려면 이 버튼을 눌러주세요.
Push this button to play the game.

16-4 기다리는 사람들에게 양보 좀 해주시겠습니까?
Will you please yield to those waiting?

16-5 이 기계는 고장 났습니다. 수리 후에 이용해주세요.
This machine is out of order. Please use after it is repaired.

17) Warm-up Area (웜업 장소)

17-1 이 테니스 코트는 당신의 레저 활동을 위해 무료로 개방되어 있습니다.
This tennis court is open to you all without charge for your leisure activities.

17-2 영수증에 사인한 후에 마음대로 테니스 라켓, 볼, 배드민턴 라켓, 그리고 셔틀콕을 마음대로 사용해도 좋습니다.
Please feel free to use tennis rackets, balls, badminton rackets, and shuttlecocks, after signing the receipt.

17-3 사용하신 후에 그것들을 제자리에 놓고 영수증과 비교해서 그것들을 체크하세요.
Please return them after use and check them against the receipt.

18) Circuit Training Center (서킷 트레이닝 센터)

Ⅳ. Attendance in the Olympics

18-1 이곳은 서킷 트레이닝 센터입니다.
This is the circuit training center.

18-2 이 센터는 당신의 운동과 피트니스를 위해 무료로 개방합니다.
This center is open to you all without charge for your physical exercise and fitness.

18-3 강사가 있습니다. 그래서 그의 지시에 따라 장비를 사용해주세요.
We have an instructor. So please use the equipment according to his instruction.

18-4 사고를 방지하기 위해 규칙을 따르세요.
Please follow the rules to prevent accidents.

19) Swimming Pool / Sauna (수영장 / 사우나)

19-1 이곳은 수영장 또는 사우나로 통하는 라커룸입니다.
This is the locker room leading to the swimming pool / sauna.

19-2 이곳은 여자만 (들어올 수 있습니다).
This is for women only.

19-3 이곳은 남자만 (들어올 수 있습니다).
This is for men only.

19-4 사고가 발생하면, 즉시 메디컬 케어 직원에게 알리세요.
When an accident occurs, please notify the medical care staff immediately.

20) Religious Hall (종교 홀)

20-1 이곳은 종교적인 방입니다.
This is the religious hall.

IV. Attendance in the Olympics

20-2 당신의 종교적인 의식은 이 홀에서 하게 되는데, 그 홀은 당신의 운동능력 향상을 위한 명상과 상담을 하도록 하루 24시간동안 개방됩니다.

Your religious ceremonies are held in this hall, which is open for 24 hours a day for meditation and counsel for the improvement of your athletic abilities.

20-3 이곳은 신교도 예배당입니다.

This is the protestant chapel.

20-4 이곳은 종교의 예배 또는 예배를 하지 않는 사람들을 위한 명상의 홀입니다. 마음대로 사용하십시오.

This is a hall of meditation for those who practise other religions or no religion. Please feel free to use it.

Ⅳ. Attendance in the Olympics

10. Games Management
(경기 운영)

1) Traffic Entrance in the Venue (경기장 입구)

Admission : 실례합니다. 저에게 당신의 AD카드 좀 보여주시겠습니까?
Excuse me, sir. Would you show me your AD card?

Foreigner : AD카드를 가지고 있진 않지만, 핸드볼경기를 관람하고 싶습니다.
I have no AD card, but I want to watch the handball game.

Admission : 죄송하지만, 여기 입구는 올림픽 가족의 통행만 됩니다.
I'm sorry, but this gate is only for the passage of the Olympic family.

Foreigner : 그러면 경기장에 들어가기 위해 어디로 가야되나요?
Then where should I go to enter the venue?

Admission : 우선 첫째로(무엇보다도) 당신은 관중의 출입을 위한 주차장에 차를 주차해야 합니다.
You must first of all park your car at the parking place for the audience entrance.

Foreigner : 관중을 위한 주차장은 어디에 있나요?
And where is the parking place for the audience?

Admission : 주차장은 여기에서 500미터 남쪽인 수송 중학교에 위치해 있습니다.
The parking place is located at the Susong Middle School 500 meters south of here.

Ⅳ. Attendance in the Olympics

Foreigner : 거긴 어떻게 가죠?
　　　　　　How can I get there?

Admission : 첫째, 당신이 오던 길로 되돌아가면 산업도로를 만나게 될 것입니다. 그 도로를 따라 남쪽으로 약 200미터 가면 주차장으로 향하는 방향표지판(도로표지판)을 찾을 것입니다.
　　　　　　First you must turn back from the way you have come and you'll meet an industrial road. Go about 200 meters south along that road and you will find a sign leading to the parking place

Foreigner : 감사합니다.
　　　　　　Thank you.

Admission : 천만에요. 당신이 경기를 관람하는 즐거운 시간을 가졌으면 합니다.
　　　　　　You're welcome. I hope you have a pleasant time watching the game.

2) Audience Information Outside of the Venue (경기장 밖 관중 안내소)

Guide : 무엇을 도와드릴까요?
　　　　What can I do for you?

Foreigner : 핸드볼 경기의 일정과 시간을 알고 싶습니다.
　　　　　　I want to know the schedule and time of the handball games.

Guide : 알겠습니다. (그에게 팜플렛을 주면서) 이 팜플렛으로부터 당신이 알고 싶은 모든 것들을 알 수 있습니다.
　　　　I see. (Presenting a pamphlet to him) You can learn from this pamphlet everything you want to know.

Foreigner : 감사합니다.
　　　　　　Thank you.

Ⅳ. Attendance in the Olympics

Guide : 더 이상 도와드릴 것이 있나요?

Is there anything further I can do for you?

Foreigner : 네, 민속품과 한국의 예절이 있는 여기에서 가까운 민속촌이 있다고 들었습니다. 거기는 어떻게 가죠?

Yes, I'm told that there is the Folk Village near here with folk products and manners of Korea. How can I go there?

Guide : 오, 민속촌! 수원에 인접한 용인에 위치해 있습니다.

Oh, the Folk Village! It is located in Yongin adjacent to Suwon.

Foreigner : 용인?

Yongin?

Guide : 네, 당신은 버스나 택시를 타고 그곳에 가야합니다.

Yes. You must take a bus or a taxi to go there.

Foreigner : 하지만 차를 가지고 있습니다.

But I have my car….

Guide : 그러면 당신은 더 쉽게 도착할 수 있습니다. 첫째, 산업도로를 따라 경부고속도로의 수원인터체인지로 운전해야 합니다. 그리고 곧장 앞으로 운전하면 민속촌으로 향하는 방향표지판(도로표지판)을 찾을 것입니다. 그 표지(신호)를 따르세요.

Then you can get there more easily. First you must drive along the industrial road to the Suwon IC of the Kyeongbu Expressway. Then drive straight ahead and you will find the road signs for the Folk Village. You may follow the signs.

Foreigner : 정말 감사합니다.

Thank you very much.

Guide : 질문이 있다면 언제든지 저희에게 물어보시고 오늘의 경기를 관

IV. Attendance in the Olympics

람하는 즐거운 시간을 가졌으면 합니다.

Refer to us whenever you gave any questions and have a pleasant time watching today's game.

3) Entrance for the Olympic Family (올림픽선수 가족을 위한 출입)

A: 실례합니다. AD카드 좀 보여주시겠어요?

Excuse me, but let me see your AD card.

B: 여기 있습니다.

Here you are.

A: 감사합니다. 여기 있습니다.

Thank you. (After seeing the AD card) Here you are.

B: 죄송하지만 VIP 룸이 어디에 있나요?

I'm sorry, but where is the VIP room?

A: VIP 룸요? 왼쪽으로 돌아가시면 첫 번째 방이 VIP 룸입니다. 각각 방은 명패가 있어 당신은 쉽게 찾을 수 있을 것입니다.

VIP room? If you turn to the left, the first room is the VIP room. Each room has its nameplate and you will find the room easily.

B: 매우 감사합니다.

Thank you very much.

4) Admission Control within the Venue (경기장내 출입 통제)

Admission : 실례합니다. 무엇을 찾으시나요?

Excuse me, sir. What are you seeking?

Foreigner : 저는 VIP휴게실로 가길 원합니다. 어디로 가야 하나요?

I want to go to VIP lounge. Where should I go?

Ⅳ. Attendance in the Olympics

Admission : 죄송하지만 저에게 AD카드 좀 보여주시겠어요?
　　　　　　I'm sorry, but would you show me your AD card?

Foreigner : 여기 있습니다.
　　　　　　Here you are.

Admission : 유감스럽지만 당신의 AD카드론 그곳을 방문할 수가 없습니다.
　　　　　　Thank you, but you cannot visit there with your AD card.

Foreigner : 오, 왜 안돼요?
　　　　　　Oh, Why not?

Admission : 당신의 AD카드로는 VIP장소를 방문하는 것이 허락되지 않아, 당신은 그곳으로 갈수 없습니다.
　　　　　　Your AD card does not allow you to visit the VIP places, so you cannot go there.

Foreigner : 그러면 제가 어떻게 해야 되나요?
　　　　　　What can I do then?

Admission : 문제가 무엇입니까? 당신을 도울 수 있다면 저에게 말씀해주세요.
　　　　　　What's the matter? Please tell me, if there is anyway I can help you.

Foreigner : 네, 경기장에서 미국의 IOC위원 Mr. Richard씨를 만나기로 되어 있습니다.
　　　　　　Yes. I'm supposed to meet with Mr. Richard, an IOC committeeman of U.S.A. in the venue.

Admission : 정말로요? 제가 확인하는 동안 잠시만 기다려주세요(IOC 위원이 지금 경기장에 있는 지를 알아보기 위해 워키토키로 의전담당관실에 통화하고 그 사람이 없다는 것을 안다.) 미안하지만, 현재 그는 경기장에 없습니다.

Are you? Please wait for a moment while I am checking.(He talks over a walkie-talkie with the Protocol Manager's to see if the IOC committeeman is in the venue at present and gets aware of his absence.). I'm sorry, but he is not in the venueat the present time.

Foreigner : 아, 그가 없다고요? 어쨌든 감사합니다.

Oh, isn't he? Thanks anyway.

Admission : 유감입니다.

I'm sorry.

5) VIP Entrance - VIP Stand (VIP출입구 - VIP관람석)

Receiving : 환영합니다. 우선, 당신의 AD카드를 확인하려고 합니다. 이 길로 나를 따라 오세요.

Welcome. For a start, we'd like to confirm your AD card. Follow me this way. please.

Admission : 실례합니다. 당신의 AD카드를 봐도 될까요?

Excuse me. May I see your AD card?

VIP : 여기 있습니다.

Here you are.

Admission : 감사합니다. 음, 지금 입구로 들어가도 좋습니다.

Thank you. (After seeing the AD card) Well, now you may enter the gate.

Receiving : 폐를 끼쳐 쇠송하지만, 방문자 기록책자에 당신의 이름을 쓰신다면 매우 감사하겠습니다.

I am sorry to trouble you, but I should be very thankful if you would enter your name in the visitors' book.

Ⅳ. Attendance in the Olympics

VIP : 여기에 사인하면 되나요?
　　　Should I sign here?

Admission : 좋습니다.(네) 감사합니다.
　　　All right. Thank you.

VIP : 이 게임 전에 어느 팀끼리 경기하였나요?
　　　What teams were playing before this one?

Guide : 지금 진행중인 경기는 한국과 일본과의 경기인데, 10시에 시작하였습니다.
　　　The game now going on is between Korea and Japan. It started at 10 o'clock.

VIP : 감사합니다.
　　　Thank you.

Guide : 이쪽으로 오세요.
　　　Come this way.

Guide 2 : 환영합니다. 핸드볼 경기장에 방문해주셔서 감사합니다. 이쪽으로 오세요.(VIP 라운지로 안내한다.) 여기에 앉으세요.
　　　Welcome. Thank you for visiting the venue of the handball games. Come this way. (Leads him to the VIP lounge.) Take a seat here, sir.

VIP : 당신의 친절에 감사합니다.
　　　Thank you for your kindness.

Guide 2 : 도와드릴 것이 있으시면 언제든지 말씀하세요.
　　　Tell me whenever there's anything I can do for you.

VIP : 그러면, 부탁드려도 될까요? (물어봐도 될까요?)
　　　Then, can I ask you a favor?

IV. Attendance in the Olympics

Guide 2 : 네. 당신이 알고 싶은 무엇이든 물어보세요.
Yes. Ask anything you want to know.

VIP : 이 게임 전에 어느 팀끼리 경기하였나요?
What teams were playing before this one?

Guide 2 : 이전 경기는 한국과 일본 팀이었습니다.
The previous game was between Korean and Japanese teams.

VIP : 오, 그래요? 저는 그 경기의 결과를 알고 싶었습니다. 저에게 결과 좀 알려주시겠어요?
Oh, was it? I'd like to know the result of the game. Would you let me know?

Guide 2 : 네. 여기서 조금만 기다리세요. 제가 컴퓨터로 처리된 경기의 결과를 가져오겠습니다.
Yes. Wait here just a moment. I will bring you the computer-processed data of the result of the game.

VIP : 만일 당신이 그것을 가져오신다면 친절함에 감사드릴 것입니다.
I would appreciate your kindness if you could do that.

Guide 2 : (잠시후 그가 자료를 가지고 돌아온다)여기 있습니다.
(A little later he returns with the data.) Here you are.

VIP : 정말 감사합니다.
Thank you so much.

Guide 2 : 제가 할 수 있는 또 다른 것이 있나요?
Is there any other thing I can do for you?

VIP : 아니요, 그것이 전부입니다. 감사합니다.
No, that's all. Thank you.

IV. Attendance in the Olympics

11. At the International Airport
(국제공항에서)

Place : 인천 국제공항
Incheon International Airport

Situation : B4축구팀의 매니저가 팀의 가이드를 만났습니다.
The manager of B4 soccer team meets with the team guide.

Guide : 안녕하세요? 저는 Mr. Park이고, 당신의 팀을 위한 가이드입니다.
How do you do, sir? I am Mr. Park, a guide for your team.

Manager : 오, 그러세요? 안녕하세요? 저는 Richard 이고 호주 팀의 매니저입니다.
Oh, are you? How do you do? I'm Richard, the manager of the Australian team.

Guide : 당신은 호주에서 한국까지 먼 거리를 여행하여 피곤함에 틀림없습니다.
You must be tired from travelling a long way from Australia to Korea. Do you like the weather in Korea?

Manager : 제가 전에 들었던 것처럼 하늘이 맑고 푸르군요. 지금 여기는 가을이네요. 그렇지 않아요?
The sky is so clear and blue as I heard before. It is autumn here now, isn't it?

Guide : 네, 맞습니다. 저희 한국 사람들은 가을을 '천고마비'의 계절 또는 하늘이 높고 말들이 살찌는 계절이라 부릅니다.
Yes, it is. We Koreans call autumn the season of 'Cheon-Go-Ma-Bee' or the season when the sky is high and the horses get fat.

Ⅳ. Attendance in the Olympics

Manager: 매우 재미(흥미)있는 표현이네요. – '하늘이 높고 말들이 살찌는 계절'
It is a very interesting expression — 'the season when the sky is high and the horses get fat'.

Guide: 당신이 오기 전에, 저는 당신 팀의 이동일정을 보기 위해 안내센터에 들렀습니다. 이 카드를 보시면, 내일 당신의 팀은 버스로 광주를 갈 것이며 광주에 있는 선수촌의 신양파크호텔에 투숙합니다.
Before you came, I dropped by the Information Center to see your team's moving schedule. (Showing a card) As you see in this card, tomorrow (the 14th) your team will go to Gwangju by bus prepared for your team's use and check into the Sinyang Park Hotel, the athletic village in Gwangju.

광주에서 당신의 팀은 9월 7일까지 내내 연습할 것이고, 9월 10일에 무등 경기장에서 첫 번째 예선경기를 하고, 9월 12일 대전에서 두 번째 경기를 하고, 그리고 9월 15일 다시 광주에서 세 번째 경기를 합니다.
In Gwangju your team will practice through September 7, and have the first preliminary game in Gwangju Mudeung Stadium on Sept. 10, the second in Daejeon on Sept. 12, and the third in Gwangju again on Sept. 15.

물론 대전 경기 때문에 당신은 아침에 광주에서 대전까지 이동해야 하고 경기가 끝난 후, 저녁에 광주로 돌아옵니다.
Of course for the Daejeon game, you must move in the morning from Gwangju to Daejeon, and in the evening, after the game, return to Gwangju.

저는 당신의 팀이 B그룹선두로 준준결승까지 나아갈 거라 믿고 (조 1위로 준준결승에 올라가면) 19일 광주로 이동해야 하고 만약 조2위이면 같은 날 대구로 이동해야합니다.

IV. Attendance in the Olympics

If your team advances to the quarterfinal match as the head of the B Group, your team will move to Gwangju on the 19, and if your team becomes the second, then you may have to move to Daegu on the same day.

그리고 만일 당신의 팀이 광주에서 준준결승을 이기면 24일 주경기장에서 준결승을 할 것이고 대구에서 준준결승을 이긴다면 같은 날 부산 구덕경기장에서 경기를 할 것입니다. 물론 결승은 10월 1일 올림픽 주경기장에서 열릴 것입니다.

And if your team wins the quarterfinal game in Gwangju, your team will have a semifinal match in the main stadium on the Sept. 24, and in case you win the Daegu quarterfinal game, you will have a semifinal match in Busan Gudeok Stadium on the same day. The final game, of course, will be held in the Olympic main stadium on October 1.

Manager: 당신의 자세한 설명에 감사드립니다. 저는 한국으로 오기 전에 일정을 알아(조사해)보았으며 한국이 우리에게 익숙하지 않아 많은 도움이 필요할 거라 생각했습니다.

Thank you for your detailed explanation. I also examined the schedule before I came to Korea, and I think we need much help from you for Korea is not familiar to us.

Guide: 당신이 필요할 때 언제든지 도움을 요청하세요. 진심으로 당신을 도울 것입니다.

Please ask for help at any time you need it. I will help you with my whole heart.

Manager: 언제까지 저희 팀을 안내해주시나요? 그리고 당신의 일정은 무엇입니까?

When do you guide our team, and what is your schedule?

IV. Attendance in the Olympics

Guide: 당신의 팀이 한국으로 들어오는 순간부터 활동을 시작하였고 한국으로 떠날 때까지입니다. 저는 당신이 머무르는 모든 기간 동안 같이 동행합니다. 공식적인 일정 통솔자로서 당신의 팀과 함께 이동할 것입니다. 물론 당신의 팀과 함께 지방도 갈 것입니다.

I go into action from the moment your team enters Korea and until you leave Korea —that is, for this whole period of your stay I will accompany you. I will move with your team as the official schedule commands. Of course I'll go to the provinces in company with your team.

Manager: 매우 감사합니다.

Thank you very much.

Guide: 자, 갑시다. 당신의 팀을 위해 공항 입구에 버스가 준비되었습니다.

Let's go. The bus is ready for your team at the entrance of the airport.

Ⅳ. Attendance in the Olympics

12. On the playing Field
(경기장에서)

Place: 광주에 있는 금호회사 경기장
Geumho Company Playing Field in Gwangju

Situation: (A그룹의 A3팀이 부산에서 예선경기를 마치고 최종연습을 위해 준준결승이 열리는 광주로 이동했다. 팀의 매니저가 상대편 나라의 국영방송 취재기자와 인터뷰하고 있다; 팀 통역가이드가 그들을 위해 통역을 한다.)

(When the A3 team of the Group A, which finished the preliminary games in Busan and transferred to Gwangju where the quarterfinal games will be held is doing the final practice, the Manager of the team is giving an interview to a newsman of the state-run broadcasting station of the counterpart country; the guide of the team interprets for them.)

Newsman: (팀가이드에게) 저희를 위해 통역 좀 해주겠어요? 저는 Brian이고, 영국 국영 방송국의 취재기자입니다.

(To the team guide) Would you interpret for us? I'm Brian, a newsman from the English state-run broadcasting station.

Guide: 네, 그러죠.
Yes, I would.

Newsman: (A3팀의 매니저에게) 당신의 팀이 A그룹의 선수로서 준준결승으로 이동했고, 지금, 당신의 팀 컨디션은 어떤가요?

(To the manager of the A3 team) As was expected your team moves to the quarterfinal match as the head of A Group, And

IV. Attendance in the Olympics

Newsman 이어서 생략 —

now, in what condition is your team?

Manager: 음, 저희는 매우 좋은 상태입니다. 마치 한국의 가을하늘 같아요.
Well, we're in very good condition. Like the autumn sky of Korea.

Newsman: 내일 당신의 팀과 맞서게 될 일본 팀에 대해 어떻게 생각하십니까?
What do you think of the Japanese team which your team will fight tomorrow?

Manager: 한마디로, 좋은 팀이죠. 그 팀은 한국과 더불어 아시아에서 강한 두 팀 중 하나입니다. 그렇지 않나요? 저는 몇 년전에, 예전의 브라질의 축구 스타였던 Maradona 가 팀의 매니저가 된 이래로 발전되었다고 들었습니다.
In a word, it is a good team. The team is one of the two strongest teams in Asia with Korea, isn't it? I'm told that it has made a great progress since, several years ago, the former soccer star Mr. Maradona of Brazil became to the team manager.

Newsman: 내일의 경기를 위해 어떤 전략을 세웠습니까?
What tactics do you plan for tomorrow's game?

Manager: 전통적으로 저희 팀은 파워, 스피드, 조직력을 기초로 두는 443전략을 가지고 있습니다. 우선 저희는 상대팀의 공격적인 리듬을 깨기 위해 미드필드에서 우위를 점할 것이고 기회가 있을 때마다 골을 넣을 것입니다. 저는 Mr. Park과 Mr. Kim의 득점력을 믿습니다.
Traditionally our team has a 443 strategy based on power, speed and organizing ability. From the first we would dominate the midfield to break the offensive rhythm of the opposite team and make a goal at any chances. I believe in the scoring competency of Mr. Park and Mr. Kim.

Newsman: 당신은 우리가 주의를 기울여야 할 필요가 있는 선수가 누구라 생

Ⅳ. Attendance in the Olympics

각하고, 그에 대한 당신의 대책은 무엇입니까?

Which player do you think we need to be cautious of, and what is your countermeasure against him?

Manager: 당신이 예상한바 미드필더 Hiroshi입니다. 그의 개인적인 기술, 스피드, 슈팅은 매우 위협적입니다. 그는 특히 예선경기에서 훌륭했고 그는 멕시코를 상대로 경기마지막 하프시간 20분에 결승골을 넣었습니다. 저희는 그를(상대선수) 묶어버리기 위해 Mr. Park에게 그를 단독 마크하도록 할 것입니다.

The mid-fielder Hiroshi, as you expected. His individual skill, speed and shooting are very threatening. He was especially great when, in a preliminary game, he kicked the winning goal into the goal of Mexico at the 20th minute of the last half of the game. We will have Mr. Park mark him exclusively to stall him.

Newsman: 당신의 팀은 부산에서 첫 번째 예선경기를 치렀고 대구에서 두 번째 경기를, 다시 부산에서 세 번째 경기를 치렀고 불과 그저께 광주에 왔습니다. 이러한 빈번한 이동이 내일의 경기에 영향을 미칠 선수들에게 어떤 나쁜 영향이 될 거라 생각하지 않으십니까?

Your team had the first preliminary game in Busan, the second in Daegu, and the third in Busan again, and moved to Gwangju only the day before yesterday. Don't you think the frequent movement gave any unfavorable harm to the players which will affect tomorrow's game?

Manager: 아니요, 결코 문제가 되지 않습니다. 저희는 좋은 예선경기를 했고 충분한 휴식을 취했습니다.

No, there is nothing to be troubled about. We had good preliminary games and had sufficient rest.

Newsman: 당신은 내일경기에서 당신의 팀이 승리할거라 확신하십니까?

IV. Attendance in the Olympics

Are you convinced of your team's victory in tomorrow's game?

Manager: 물론 저희는 이길 것이고 준결승을 위해 모레 태릉스포츠파크에서 가볍게 몸을 풀 것입니다.

Of course we will win, and the day after tomorrow will warm up lightly in Taeneung Sports Park for the semi-final game.

Newsman: 그리고 마지막 질문입니다: B1팀이 경기에서 이길 거라 생각하십니까?

And this is my last question: Do you think the B1 team can win the game

Manager: (미소를 띠며) 글쎄요, 볼이 둥글다고 합니다만….

(With a smile) Well, they say the ball is round, but….

IV. Attendance in the Olympics

13. In a Team Bus
(팀 버스 안에서)

Place: 선수촌에 있는 팀 버스 안에서(지방으로 이동을 위해)
In a team bus(for transferring to the province) at the athletes village.

Situation: 브라질 축구팀의 매니저 펠레와 가이드 홍길동간의 대화. (9월 15일 21시, 브라질 팀이 전용기로 한국으로 들어왔고, 9월 20일 10시까지 서울 선수촌에서 지냈고 12시에 예선경기가 개최될 대구로 출발할 준비가 되어있다. 그들은 선수촌에서 홍길동을 만난다.)
The conversation between Manager Pele of the Brazilian soccer team and its guide, Mr. Hong Gil Dong. (The Brazilian team, having entered Korea on Sept. 15 at 21:00 by a team plane and spent the night at the athletes village in Seoul, by 10:00 on Sept. 20, had made ready to depart at 12:00, for Daegu where the preliminary games will be held. They meet Mr. Hong at the athletes village.)

Hong: 좋은 아침입니다, 선생님. 비행기로 먼 여행을 하셨는데 피로가 풀리셨습니까?
Good morning, sir. Are you recovered from the long trip by plane?

Manger: 선수촌의 시설이 매우 좋고 방이 잠을 자는데 너무 편안했습니다.
The facilities in the village were excellent and the room was very comfortable to sleep in.

Hong: 대구로 갈 모든 준비가 되었습니까? 약 10분전에 당신의 팀 버스가 주차장에 도착했습니다.

IV. Attendance in the Olympics

Are you all ready for transferring to Daegu? About ten minutes ago your team bus arrived at the parking lot.

Manger: 네, 저희는 모든 준비되었습니다. 갑시다. (선수들과 같이 미스터 홍과 브라질 팀의 매니저가 주차장으로 걸어갑니다.)
Yes, we are all ready. Let's go (Mr. Hong and the manager of the Brazilian team, along with the players, go on foot to the parking lot.)

Hong: 이 버스가 우리를 대구로 데려다 줄 것입니다. 자, 타세요.
This bus is the one that will transport us to Daegu. Let's get on it.

Manger: 서울에서 대구까지 얼마나 멀고 거기에 도착하는데 얼마나 걸리죠?
How far is it from Seoul to Daegu and how long does it take to go there?

Hong: 약 300km이고 당신이 길에서 20분 쉰다고 해도 4시간이 채 안 걸립니다.(4시간보다 적게 걸린다) 대구로 가는 길에 서울로부터 150km 밑에 있는 대전이 있고, 부산은 대구 남방 면 140km에 있고 1시간 30분 거리입니다.
It is about 300 kms, and, even if you take a 20 minute rest on the way, it takes no longer than 4 hours. On the way to Daegu is Daejeon at the spot 150 kms down from Seoul, and Busan is at 140 kms south of Daegu — that is a distance of one and a half hours.

Manger: 저는 예선 경기가 서울뿐만 아니라 부산, 대구, 광주에서 개최될 거라고 들었습니다. 대구에 대해 말해주세요.
I'm told that preliminary games will be held in Busan, Daegu, and Gwangju as well as in Seoul. Tell me about Daegu.

Hong: 대구는 2백만 인구로 한국에서 3번째로 큰 도시입니다. 오래전부터

Ⅳ. Attendance in the Olympics

교육의 도시로 불려졌고 최근에 방직산업을 우선으로 산업이 많이 발전했습니다. 방직제품은 전자제품과 함께 한국의 수출품으로 크게 중요해졌습니다.

Daegu is the third largest city in Korea with the population of 2 million. It has been called a city of education from old times, and in recent times has developed much industry with priority given to the textile industry. The textile goods are of greatest importance along with the electronic goods in the export items of Korea.

Manger: 오, 알겠습니다. 브라질에 대해 시민들에게는 어떻게 알려져 있나요?

Oh, I see. How is Brazil recognized to the citizens?

Hong: 거의 모든 대구시민들에게는 브라질이 축구와 커피의 나라로 알려져 있습니다. 최근에 브라질은 주변의 철강 산업을 중심으로 산업들을 발전시키고 있습니다. 게다가, 풍부한 자원과 큰 성장 잠재력을 가지고 있어 한국의 좋은 동반자가 될 수 있습니다.

Brazil is known as the country of soccer and coffee to almost all the citizens. Recently Brazil was active in developing industries centering around the steel industry. Besides, it has abundant resources and a big potential of growth, and thus it could be a good partner of Korea.

Manger: 감사합니다. 저는 대구시민들을 실망시키지 않도록 좋은 경기를 해야 한다고 생각합니다.

Thank you. I think we should play the best games not to dissatisfy the citizens of Daegu.

Hong: 저는 당신의 팀이 확실히 우리에게 좋은 경기를 보여줄 거라 믿습니다. 오, 지금 우리에게 대구를 소개하기 위해 비디오가 켜졌습니다. 저것을 보면서 이야기를 계속 나누죠.

IV. Attendance in the Olympics

I believe your team certainly will show us good games. Oh, now the video is on to introduce Daegu to us. Let's watch it and continue talking.

Manger: 가장 좋아하는 한국 선수가 누구입니까?
Who's your favorite Korean player?

Hong: 제가 가장 좋아하는 선수요? 박지성 선수를 가장 좋아해요. 최고의 공격수이지요. 빠르고, 집중력있고, 그리고 열심히 노력하거든요. 항상 자세가 되어 있어요.
My favorite player? I like Ji-Sung Park best. He is the best playmaker. He is fast, concentrated and strenuous. He always has the right attitude and mentality.

Manger: 그런데, 이 초청권은 어디서 구했어요?
By the way, where did you get these comp tickets?

Hong: 초청권이 아니고 제가 온라인으로 산거예요.
Well, they're not complimentary tickets, I bought them online.

Manger: 뭐라고요? 이 경기를 보려고 2장을 샀어요?
You what? You bought two tickets to come to the game?

Hong: 예, 여자 친구랑요.
Yes, with my girlfriend.

Manger: 내일 오후에 시간 있으세요?
Are you free tomorrow afternoon?

Hong: 사정에 따라 다르죠. 왜요?
It depends. Why do you ask?

Manger: 우리 팀을 데리고 한국과 일본 4강전 경기를 보려가려고 하는데 같이 갈래요?

IV. Attendance in the Olympics

I'd like to take my team to the quarterfinal game of Korea vs. Japan. Would you like to come with me?

Hong: 그럼요. 제가 박지성의 왕 팬입니다. 몇 시에 경기가 시작하죠?
Sure. I am a great fan of Ji-Sung Park. What time does the game start?

Manger: 3시에 시작하지만, 늦어도 2시 30분까지는 가야돼요.
It starts at 3:00 pm, but we need to be there no later than 2:30.

Hong: 알겠습니다. 같이 가겠습니다. 그런데, 게임을 어디서 하죠?
I see. I'll accompany you. By the way, where is the game?

Manger: 팜플렛을 보니까 광주월드컵 경기장에서요.
The Pamphlet says it's in Gwangju World Cup Stadium.

IV. Attendance in the Olympics

14. At the Ticket Office
(매표소에서)

Place: 잠실 경기장에 있는 매표소
The ticket office at the Jamsil Stadium

Situation: (잠실 경기장 매표소 근처에서 두 외국인이 입장권을 사기위해 이리 저리 걷고 있다. 매표소에 있는 가이드가 그것을 보고 두 외국에게 다가간다.)

(By the ticket window at the Jamsil Stadium two foreigners are going here and there to find out how to buy the tickets. A guide at the ticket office, seeing that, approaches the two foreigners.)

Guide: 무엇을 도와드릴까요?
May I help you?

Foreigner: 오, 도와주세요. 저는 스페인에서 온 Marsha입니다.(그는 영어가 서툴렀다.)
Oh, yes please. I am Marsha from Spain. (She is poor in English.)

Guide: 안녕하세요? 잠시만 기다려주세요. 죄송하지만 제가 스페인어를 못합니다. 제가 스페인어를 잘하는 가이드에게 도움을 요청할게요. (잠시 후, 스페인어통역사가 온다.)
How do you do? Wait a while. Excuse me, but I don't speak Spanish. I will ask for help of the guide who speaks Spanish well. (After a while, the interpreter of the Spanish language comes.)

Interpreter: 무엇을 도와드릴까요?

Ⅳ. Attendance in the Olympics

What can I do for you?

Foreigner: 네, 저희는 스페인과 이탈리아 경기입장권을 사고 싶습니다.
Yes. We want to buy tickets for the game between Spain and Italy.

Interpreter: (가이드에게 물어본 후에.) 입장권은 2가지 종류가 있습니다. - 1등석과 2등석. 1등석 비용은 100,000원이고 2등석 비용은 50,000원입니다.
(After asking the guide.) There are two kinds of tickets — the first-class and the second-class. The first-class costs 100,000 won each, the second 50,00 won.

Foreigner: 저희는 1등석 2장을 원합니다. (그들은 티켓을 산 후에...)
We want two first-class tickets.(After they buy the tickets.)

Interpreter: 1등석 좌석 출입구는 3번과 8번 입구입니다. 당신은 오른쪽에 있는 메인입구를 통해 가시는 게 좋고 3번 입구로 들어가세요. 제가 길을 안내해드리겠습니다. (3번 입구로 안내하면서)
The entrance for the first-class seats are gate No. 3 and 8. You'd better go through the main gate on the right and enter by the Gate 3. I will lead the way for you. (Leading the way to the Gate 3)

Foreigner: 감사합니다.
Thank you.

Interpreter: 경기는 19:00에 시작합니다. 좋은 시간 보내시고 스페인이 이기길 바랍니다.
The game begins at 19:00. Have a pleasant time and I wish you a victory for Spain.

Foreigner: 정말 감사합니다.
Thank you very much.

IV. Attendance in the Olympics

15. In a Hotel Lobby
(호텔 로비에서)

Miss A: 안녕하세요. 구름이 약간 낀 날씨입니다.

Good morning. It's a little cloudy today.

VIP: 비가 올 것 같아 보이지 않군요. 그렇죠? 오늘의 경기에 대해 궁금합니다. 여자 자유형 100m 결승이 올림픽파크 수영장에서 열리죠. 수영(경기)에 대해 관심있는 모든 사람들이 결과에 관심을 가지겠죠. 저는 중국 수영선수가 지금 두각을 나타내고 있다고 들었어요.

It doesn't seem to rain, does it? I feel curious about today's match. Women's 100 freestyle final is to be held at the swimming pool in the Olympic Park. Everyone concerned with swimming is interested in the result. I hear a Chinese swimmer is standing out at this time.

Miss A: 어제 그것을 TV에서 잠깐 봤었습니다. 자동차가 준비되면 그 곳으로 갑시다.

I watched a little bit of that on TV yesterday. Let's go there when the car is ready.

VIP: 네, 갑시다.

Yes, let's go.

Miss A: 차가 안 보입니다. 잠시만 기다려주시겠어요? 제가 교통부서와 의전부에 물어보고 곧바로 시정(조정)하겠습니다.
(그녀가 그것에 관해 교통과 의전부서에 요청한다.)

But I can't see the car. Would you wait for a moment, please? I'll check with the transportation and the protocol for that and arrange the matter soon.(She inquires of the Transportation and the Protocol

IV. Attendance in the Olympics

about it.)

VIP: 괜찮습니다. 왜냐하면 몇 분 뒤에 진행되기 때문입니다.
I think it's all right, because the match allows me a few minutes.

Miss A: 자동차가 저기 있습니다! 제가 먼저 타겠습니다.
There's the car! I'll get in first.

VIP: 당신은 잘 훈련된 안내원입니다. 왜냐하면 이와 같은 어려운 상황에서 당황하지 않고 잘 행동하기 때문입니다.
You are a well-trained escort, for you are not embarrassed at a difficult situation like this and manage it properly.

Miss A: 이곳이 수영경기장입니다. VIP를 위한 입구는 이쪽입니다. 이 입구로 들어가세요. 경기 후에, 의전담당원에게 저에게 전화하도록 하면 제가 바로 입구에서 기다릴 것입니다. 자, 그러면 안내원 방에서 기다리겠습니다.(기다리는 동안, 그녀는 다음 방문할 것에 대해 계획하고 운전기사와 만날 장소를 잡고 의전부서에 보고했습니다.)
This is the swimming venue. The entrance for the VIPs is this way. Please enter by this gate. After the match, please have the Protocol member call me, and I'll be at the entrance gate soon. Well, then I'll wait in the waiting room of the escorts. (While waiting, she plans for the next visit, makes sure of the meeting place with the driver, and reports to the Protocol Department.)

VIP: (경기가 끝난 직후, VIP와 안내원이 다시 만나) Miss A, 중국 수영선수가 우승했어요. 매우 극적이었고 관중들이 그녀에게 큰 박수와 찬사를 보냈어요.
(Soon after the match is finished, and the VIP and the escort meet again.) Miss A, the Chinese swimmer won the victory. It was so dramatic and all the spectators gave her a big applause and cheers.

Ⅳ. Attendance in the Olympics

Miss A: 저는 인류의 진보와 화해를 스포츠만이 만들 수 있다고 생각합니다. 우리의 젊은 사람들은 스포츠를 통해 인류의 평화와 복지를 달성해야 합니다.

I think the reconciliation and the progress of mankind can be made only by sports. We young people should achieve peace and welfare of mankind through sports.

Miss A: 우리의 차가 점검하러 정비소에 들렀다 온다고 합니다. 저는 5분 내로 오겠습니다. 잠시만 기다려 주십시오.

They say our car will come after stopping by the Maintenance Center for a checkup. I'll arrive within five minutes. So you may wait just a little longer.

[참고문헌]

김기관(2004). Sean Kim's Golf English. 도서출판 예가 : 서울
김민영(2001). 영어표현 12000. 인터미디어: 서울.
김춘근(2008). 네이티브 영어로 체육수업하기. 대경북스: 서울.
능률NEAT연구소(2012). The Neat Essential. 능률교육: 서울.
오성식(1995). 오성식 생활영어. 고려원: 서울.
오응수·박정준·이순환(2011). Step by Step 스포츠 영어. HS 미디어: 서울.
이보영·아이작(2002). Talk about Sports. 넥서스 : 서울
이홍훈 외(1988). Olympic English. 서울올림픽대회조직위원회.
서성기(1999). 스포츠 잉글리시. 한영문화사 : 서울
전라남도교육청(2007). 글로벌시대 적응을 위한 스포츠 영어회화.
정의권 외(1999). 현대인의 스포츠 영어. 21세기교육사: 서울.
최영옥(1984). 체육학영어강독. 선일문화사: 서울.
최지규(1996). 한국학교 생활영어. 태성출판사: 서울.
Anthony Saba, et al.(2002). Soccer English. 형설출판사: 서울.
Jack C. Richards, et al.(2005). Person to Person. Oxford Press: New York.
Scott Fisher, Brian Stuart(2006). Speaking for Everyday Life. Darakwon: Seoul.
Web text: www.google.com
www.incheon2014.kr/인천아시아경기대회조직위원회.
www.olympic.org

[저자약력]

박 진 성(朴眞成)

- 부산대학교 체육교육과 및 동 대학원 졸업(이학박사)
- 미국 Missouri University-Columbia 방문교수
- 1988서울올림픽대회 본부 호텔 VIP영어통역
- 2015광주유니버시아드 통역 봉사자 영어교육교재 집필 위원장
- 순천대학교 인문예술대학장
- 순천대학교 사회체육학과 교수
- 현) 국립순천대학교 총장

문 한 식(文瀚植)

- 순천대학교 사회체육학과 및 교육대학원 졸업(교육학석사)
- 경상대학교 대학원 졸업(이학박사)
- 2010 호주 Victoria University Post-Doc
- 2015광주유니버시아드 통역봉사자 영어교육교재 집필위원
- 현) 순천대학교 사회체육학과 교수